# DONALYN MILLER & COLBY SHARP

W9-CCN-743

# GAME CHANGER!

## Book Access for All Kids

SCHOLASTIC

*To my mom, who always made sure I had a library card.*
—DM


*To Alaina, who fills my life with endless stories.*
—CS

Photos ©: cover top and throughout: Africa Studio/Shutterstock; cover bottom and throughout: smartboy10/Getty Images; 10: vasabii/Shutterstock; 29 top: Microba Grandioza/Shutterstock; 29 center top: mattjeacock/iStockphoto; 29 center: aklionka/Shutterstock; 29 center bottom: arbuz/Shutterstock; 29 bottom: alekseiveprev/Shutterstock; 29 composite: Jennifer Lagarde; 81-84: Brad Gustafson; 131, 132: Becky Calzada; all other images by Marta Xochilt Perez.

Credits: page 10: "Books Make a Difference in Kids' Lives" infographic copyright © 2013 by First Book. Used by permission of First Book; page 13: "Summer Reading Loss" infographic copyright © 2015 by Reading Is Fundamental. Used by permission of Reading Is Fundamental; page 68: "Social Identity Wheel" graphic adapted from material created for "Voices of Discovery" by Intergroup Relations Center, Arizona State University. Copyright © 2018 by Arizona State University. Used by permission of Intergroup Relations Center, Arizona State University.

Scholastic is not responsible for the content of third-party websites and does not endorse any site or imply that the information on the site is error-free, correct, accurate, or reliable.

Publisher/Content Editor: Lois Bridges
Editorial director: Sarah Longhi
Development editor: Raymond Coutu
Production editor: Danny Miller
Art director: Brian LaRossa
Interior designer: Maria Lilja

No part of this publication may be reproduced in whole or in part, or stored in a retrieval system, or transmitted in any form or by any means, electronic, mechanical, photocopying, recording, or otherwise, without written permission of the publisher. For information regarding permission, write to Scholastic Inc., 557 Broadway, New York, NY 10012.

Copyright © 2018 by Donalyn Miller and Colby Sharp.
All rights reserved. Published by Scholastic Inc.
Printed in the USA.

ISBN-13: 978-1-338-31059-7
ISBN-10: 1-338-31059-3

SCHOLASTIC and associated logos are trademarks and/or registered trademarks of Scholastic Inc.
Other company names, brand names, and product names are the property and/or trademarks of their respective owners. Scholastic does not endorse any product or business entity mentioned herein.

Scholastic is constantly working to lessen the environmental impact of our manufacturing processes.
To view our industry-leading paper procurement policy, visit www.scholastic.com/paperpolicy.

1 2 3 4 5 6 7 8 9 10        40        27 26 25 24 23 22 21 20 19 18

Scholastic Inc., 557 Broadway, New York, NY 10012

# Contents

# Introduction

Children and adolescents need meaningful and consistent access to books at school and home. When they have access to books, they read more and they read better. Period. It's not groundbreaking, but it's true.

However, while schools rush to implement "personalized learning platforms" and "one-to-one laptop initiatives," we still haven't figured out how to get a paperback in every child's backpack. Decades of research have proven that book access influences students' learning outcomes, yet often we're left having to defend our position. How can we expect young people to become enthusiastic, capable readers if they don't have anything of value or relevance to read?

Too many children live in "book deserts," without consistent access to quality books (Neuman & Moland, 2016). Even children with some access often live in de facto book deserts, where all reading is controlled and managed by adults, offering them few opportunities to connect with reading. Unfortunately, book access at school and home remains inconsistent—disproportionately affecting marginalized children in rural and urban communities. There are many factors contributing to this inequity, including the defunding of school librarian positions, the lack of institutional support for school and classroom libraries, obstacles that prevent public library use, instructional methods that undermine children's positive reading experiences, standardized-testing mandates, and a lack of family support for reading.

As elementary and middle school classroom teachers, we have witnessed the power of book access to improve children's reading confidence and competence. Access to dynamic school libraries and degreed librarians influences students' academic achievement and how they feel about reading. Thoughtfully curated and well-organized classroom libraries ensure necessary instructional resources for teachers and engaging literacy invitations for children. And when children own books and library cards, they see themselves as readers. Book access is a game changer for kids.

It is going to take all of us to guarantee children's book access. Through research, testimonials from a wide range of voices in the field, instructional moves, rituals and routines, and our own classroom experiences, we hope to provide you with the tools and information you need to increase children's meaningful access to books and to launch or sustain book access initiatives in your communities.

## We hope this book will:

- Build consensus for the importance of meaningful book access for children.
- Increase institutional support for school and public libraries and librarians.
- Nurture children's positive reading identities, reading engagement, and academic growth.
- Increase access to and use of diverse children's and young adult literature, as well as an appreciation for its role in children's literacy development.
- Offer suggestions for fostering independent reading habits at school and home.
- Provide educators and families with resources for launching and sustaining effective reading communities.

We have dedicated our professional lives to learning what it takes for children and adolescents to become engaged readers, removing obstacles preventing readers' self-efficacy, and developing teaching practices that influence their reading development and interest. We have a lot of knowledge and experiences, but they don't represent the knowledge and experiences of every educator, reader, or community. Building a case for the importance of reading at school and home requires a range of voices speaking from many perspectives to convince others that reading is important to every child in every community.

We invited a number of inspirational and progressive teachers, librarians, administrators, scholars, caregivers, authors, and readers to share their experiences, ideas, and resources for improving book access and literacy opportunities for children. We are grateful to them for taking time from their own work to add their voices to this conversation. We know it is a better book because of their ideas. We invite you to add your voices to this conversation, too. Thank you for your commitment to the children and families we all serve. Together we can provide every child with the book access and literacy opportunities they deserve.

—Donalyn Miller and Colby Sharp

# From Book Deserts to Book Floods: Tools for Transformation

*"Access to books and the encouragement of the habit of reading: these two things are the first and most necessary steps in education… It is our children's right and it is also our best hope and their best hope for the future."*

**—MICHAEL MORPURGO**

See Donalyn and Colby discuss the importance of book access at scholastic.com/ GameChanger Resources

W e want children to live in "book floods" with "fingertip access to books" (Allington & McGill-Franzen, 2013). Children need books in their classrooms (Worthy & Roser, 2010; Tatum, 2009), school libraries staffed by degreed librarians (Kachel & Lance, 2013), access to public libraries (Krashen, Lee, & McQuillan, 2012), and book ownership at home (Neuman & Celano, 2012). Unfortunately, many children—disproportionately children of color living in urban and rural communities—live in book "deserts" (Neuman & Moland, 2016) without meaningful, consistent access to books at school, at home, or in their communities.

According to findings from a longitudinal study of 27 countries over 20 years, there is a direct correlation between access to books and the level of schooling children attain. Children with access to a 500-book library over the course of their childhoods benefited just as much as those growing up in homes with college-educated parents—gaining an additional 3.2 years of education on average

(Evans, et al., 2014). We don't have to provide every home with 500 books, but we need to keep in mind that book ownership paired with school libraries and public libraries can go a long way toward providing young readers with the access they need.

This gap in book access perpetuates inequities between low-income students and their middle-income peers. While schools implement intervention programs such as computer-based reading management platforms, intensive test prep, and summer school, there is little evidence such programs have a long-term positive effect on children's reading achievement and reading motivation (Allington & McGill-Franzen, 2013). Yet, study after study proves that physical access to books makes the difference. It affects young people's reading achievement (Neuman & Celano, 2012) and their motivation to read (Guthrie, 2008). It might not be groundbreaking, but giving kids access to books remains one of the most important ways to ensure they attend school with the tools they need to be successful.

In spite of all of the leaps made in education over the decades, we have never been able to provide all children with meaningful, consistent book access 365 days a year. How can we change that? How can we increase young people's access to books in schools, communities, and homes, and guarantee our children continue to have that access? This is a complex problem to solve because each community has distinct needs and concerns. No one solution will suffice, but something has to change. **Without access to books, the persistent gap between children who have access and those who don't will remain. Our students will not reach their full potential without books, regardless of the educational reforms schools implement.** Who does it benefit to provide some children with book access and not others?

While education reformers blame teachers and administrators for the middle-of-the-pack rankings of American schoolchildren on international comparisons, they fail to recognize the root cause: too many American children live in poverty (Children's Defense Fund, 2015) without consistent access to health care, nutritious food, and books. Factoring for poverty, American school children perform as well on standardized tests as children anywhere else (Carnoy & Rothstein, 2013). Without continuous, institutional support for improving book access, it is unlikely reading achievement scores will ever increase.

# The Reality of Poverty

Children in poverty are **less** likely to:

- Begin school with adequate early childhood literacy experiences such as read-alouds and academic vocabulary exposure.

- Attend schools with experienced, certified teachers and librarians.

- Attend schools with adequate school and classroom libraries.

- Live in neighborhoods with public libraries and bookstores.

- Own books.

Children in poverty are **more** likely to:

- Receive literacy instruction delivered through test-prep workbooks, scripted programs, textbooks, and worksheets instead of authentic literature.*

- Experience gaps in schooling because of unstable housing, unemployment, and illness.

- Drop out of high school with poor literacy skills.

*Lesley Morrow defines authentic text as "a stretch of real language produced by a real speaker or writer for a real audience and designed to convey a real message of some sort." Unlike contrived text, authentic text is never written or assembled for the purpose of teaching reading or delivering a set of skills (Bridges, 2018).

Children from middle-income homes may have as many as 10 regular places in their daily lives to access a new book to read, including classroom and school libraries, public libraries, brick-and-mortar bookstores, online book outlets, book fairs, and subscriptions. Conversely, children from lower-income homes may have only one or two places they can find a book to read—their school and public libraries. The book access we offer children in school must be as varied, relevant, current, and engaging as possible. For many children, school offers the only access opportunities in their lives, so it has to count.

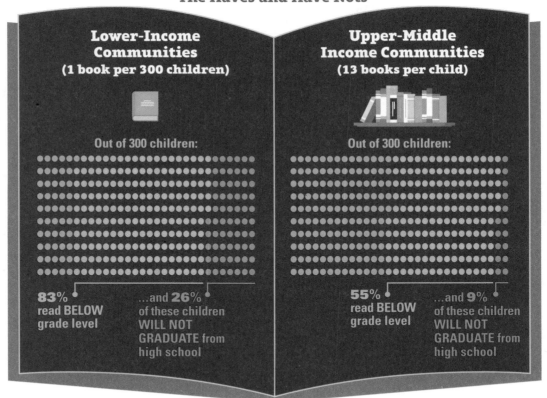

## Books Make a Difference in Kids' Lives
### The Haves and Have Nots

**Lower-Income Communities**
(1 book per 300 children)

Out of 300 children:

**83%** read BELOW grade level

...and **26%** of these children WILL NOT GRADUATE from high school

**Upper-Middle Income Communities**
(13 books per child)

Out of 300 children:

**55%** read BELOW grade level

...and **9%** of these children WILL NOT GRADUATE from high school

Differential Access to Books
(Neuman & Celano, 2012)

# Barriers to Library Use

As educators, it is frustrating when students arrive in our classrooms in the fall and admit they didn't read anything over the summer. Why didn't their caregivers take them to the public library? After all, it's free! But for many of the families we serve, access to the public library isn't "free." Not every family has a utility bill or lease in their name to show as proof of residency when applying for a library card. For families living paycheck to paycheck, the risk of library fines and fees may hinder children's library use because caregivers worry about paying for lost, damaged, or late materials. Some families avoid registering at municipal institutions such as libraries because they fear that information about their families (such as their address and ages) they provide will be shared with government agencies. Additional barriers preventing some families from using the public library include limited library hours due to budget cuts, home language differences, and transportation needs.

Forging relationships between schools and public libraries broadens the literacy, academic, and social resources we can provide our students and their families. If we want families to become active library patrons, we have to foster relationships between families and the library. Passing out library card sign-up forms at school registration time or your annual literacy night isn't going to do the job. Instead, invite public librarians to a staff meeting to share the resources they offer library patrons—including ebook and audiobook resources, homework and tutoring services, story time and craft programs, research databases, book clubs, Internet and computer access, summer reading events, and adult literacy and English-learning programs.

Children who struggle to acquire strong literacy skills often have caregivers who struggle, too. But few school districts have resources or programs to remediate adults who need literacy instruction and support. If we can connect adults in need with a literacy program through the local library, we can change the trajectory of the entire family. When an adult's literacy skills improve, it influences every child in the home.

Promote the local library during conferences and meetings. Share resources offered by your public library in school newsletters and websites. Celebrate children who acquire library cards. Work to determine the obstacles preventing some families from using the library. Is your library closed some nights or weekend days? What identification does your library system require to get a library card? What fines and fees are typically charged? Where is the library located? How hard is it to reach on foot or by public transportation? Collaborate with your local library to develop ways to overcome those obstacles.

# Rethinking Library Fines

In May 2017, the New York Public Library system discovered that blocking checkout privileges for patrons who owed $15 or more in fines prevented 20 percent of New York City children who had library cards from borrowing books (Dwyer, 2017). The president of the New York Public Library, Anthony W. Marx, knows that children who are poor lose book access more often than children who are not because of such policies. He says, "People talk about the moral hazard. But there's also a moral hazard in teaching poor kids that they will lose privileges to read, and that kids who can afford fines will not." As a result of this audit, the New York Public Library system announced a one-time amnesty for all children under the age of 18 who owed library fines (Platt, 2017).

At school, library fines often prevent children from checking out books for years because their record follows them from campus to campus as they move through school. One of Donalyn's sixth graders, Josh, was unable to check out library books because he had lost a copy of *Charlotte's Web* in third grade. His mother was unwilling or unable to pay for the book's replacement (library bound editions cost much more than trade editions), so Josh had not checked out a school library book since he was eight years old. When Josh's class went to the school library for books, Josh couldn't participate. Josh did not own many books at home or have a public library card. That single fine blocked Josh's primary source of book access—his school library. Beyond access, imagine the effect on Josh's reading identity when, week after week *for years*, he was reminded he couldn't check out any library books.

We understand the importance of returning library materials and giving children appropriate consequences for failing to follow school rules and policies, but not when it warps their reading identity development or cuts off their access. In some schools, children can shelve books, read to younger children, or write reviews for the library database to work off their fines. Other schools have stopped charging library fines altogether. Consider methods that build relationships with children and promote positive interactions with the library, librarians, and books.

# Summer Reading

Whether they live in lower socio-economic circumstances or more affluent ones, children make similar gains during the school year. They receive your high-quality instruction, the intervention and social supports your school provides, and access to resources such as books and technology. During the summer, children from middle-income homes still make incremental gains because they are attending summer camp, going on vacations, visiting museums, zoos, and libraries, and have more books and technology at home. Children who do not have those enrichment opportunities may lose as much as three months of reading growth over the summer, and that loss is cumulative—creating a widening gap between children who do not read much over the summer and children who do (Kim, 2004). Eighty percent of the achievement gap between middle-income and lower-income children accrues during the summers (Alexander, Entwisle, & Olson, 2007). No matter what gains children make during the school year, if they don't read over the summer, their learning stalls or regresses (Cooper, Borman, & Fairchild, 2010).

## SUMMER READING LOSS

More than 80 percent of children from economically disadvantaged communities can lose one to three months of reading skills over the summer.

● Students from higher economic backgrounds
● Students from lower economic backgrounds

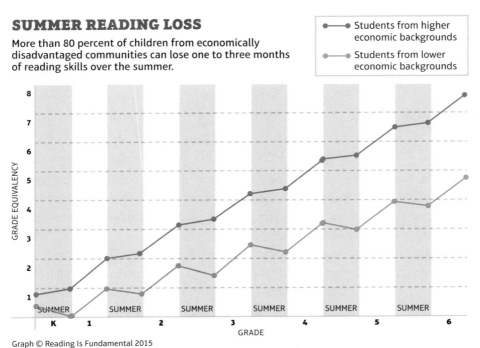

Graph © Reading Is Fundamental 2015

Source: Alexander, K. L., D. R. Entwisle, and L. S. Olson. 2007. "Lasting Consequences of Summer Learning Gap." *American Sociological Review* 72(4): 167–80; professional presentation by Dr. Alexander, February 12, 2015.

According to Scholastic's 2016 *Kids and Family Reading Report*, only 48 percent of parents surveyed knew about summer reading loss—59 percent in higher-income families and 38 percent in lower-income families. Families need to know in clear terms that if their children do not read over the summer they will lose reading skills and fall behind their same-age peers. In addition to providing information about the summer slide, we must help families overcome issues preventing their children from reading during the summer. The primary source of reading material for students in every demographic group remains school. When schools close in the summer, many children lose their only access to books.

Since reading is the only activity consistently linked to summer learning (Kim & Quinn, 2013), we must make sure all children have book access over the summer. In the primary years, kindergarten through second grade, children need to read 12 to 15 books to offset summer reading loss. For older children, from third grade through high school, reading four or five books prevents significant reading skill decline (Kim, 2004). Why the difference in age groups? Well, books for young children tend to be short and can often be read in one sitting. Books for older children are usually longer and can require several days to complete.

As parents and teachers, we have participated in every type of summer reading program possible—such as programs that incentivized reading with prizes and certificates, included community book swaps, required summer reading lists and assignments, and kept school libraries open throughout the summer. While these initiatives met the needs of some children in our communities, not one met the needs of all of them.

## Boosting Book Distribution Programs

The most effective summer reading programs put books into children's hands *before* vacation begins. Summer book distribution programs and long-term checkouts from school and classroom libraries guarantee that every child leaves school with at least a few options to read over the break.

Richard Allington and Anne McGill-Franzen (2013) conducted a longitudinal study of the effects of summer book distribution programs for low-income children. Working with 17 elementary schools with 85 percent of students receiving free and reduced lunch, the researchers created a program inviting first and second graders to select 12 to 15 books to read over the summer. After three years, they found that children who participated in the program had lower summer reading loss, higher reading assessment scores, and greater motivation and interest in reading. Students' gains matched or surpassed the benefits of summer school and cost significantly less. Indeed, they found that "…providing self-selected books for summer reading produced as much or more reading growth as attending summer school! For the poorest children the effect of our summer book distribution was twice as large as attending summer school." Children were allowed to keep the books they chose, and for many of them, those books were the only ones they owned (and, in some cases, their families owned). **Book ownership plays an important role in developing children's ownership of reading. Imagine the difference for children when they are encouraged to select books and take them home for keeps.**

Stacey Riedmiller, a fourth-grade teacher from Indiana, discovered her students owned few books and didn't have library cards. "Never assume all of your students have full access to books when they leave your building. During my first year of teaching, I had my students complete reading logs every night. One of my students logged *Hop on Pop* every single night. When I checked in with her, I found out that it was the only children's book in her home. I was shocked. How did families not have abundant books for their kids at home? How did they not have a library card? My own privilege smacked me in the face. Just because I had books and a library card when I was a child, I assumed all children did. It was a hard lesson to learn, but it was one I learned quickly."

So Stacey partnered with her school librarian and colleagues to launch a literacy initiative increasing students' book access. "We organized book giveaways throughout the school year and at the end of the school year before summer break. We started a program called Books on Blankets where we host two read-alouds each week and give out books. And now, we're working to get a vehicle so we can bring books directly to the kids of our community."

We've learned from working with school districts that the cost of books can be a significant barrier to implementing summer distribution programs. However, those districts are already spending money on summer school. Summer school programs require funding for certified teaching staff, facility use, instructional materials, transportation, and school supplies. Schools can purchase books for distribution programs for less than summer school costs. **There is little evidence that summer school programs have a lasting effect on children's reading development, but research supports the effectiveness of book distribution programs. Given our limited resources, we should use them in ways that actually benefit kids.**

# The Negative Effects of Reading Incentives and Competitions

(Adapted from Donalyn's Book Whisperer blog post, "Reading Is Its Own Reward: Summer Reading and the 7th Annual #Bookaday Challenge," May 4, 2015)

Concerned about students' summer reading, many educators and caretakers employ reading incentives and competitions to motivate children to read more. However, those well-meaning folks may be unaware of the negative long-term effects of such rewards.

A meta-analysis of 128 studies on the effects of rewards concludes, "Tangible rewards tend to have a substantially negative effect on intrinsic motivation. Even when tangible rewards are offered as indicators of good performance, they typically decrease intrinsic motivation for interesting activities" (Deci, Koestner, & Ryan, 2001). Readers motivated for personal reasons are more likely to remain invested than readers who are externally motivated through rewards (Marinak & Gambrell, 2008).

In his landmark book, *Punished by Rewards* (1995), Alfie Kohn describes why reading rewards undermine attempts to engage children with reading: "What matters more than the fact that children read is why they read and how they read. With incentive-based programs, the answer to 'why' is 'to get rewards,' and this, as the data make painfully clear, is often at the expense of interest in reading itself." Short-term reading excitement for an award or prize does not spark long-term reading engagement.

**Reading contests can harm students' reading self-efficacy and interest. Why would we employ reading initiatives that derail young readers' intrinsic motivation to read and divide them into reading winners and losers?** I have never met an adult who became a lifelong reader because they won a theme park pass or a T-shirt. Many kids around the country admit to us that they stretch the number of pages, books, and minutes they record in summer reading logs, so they can win a prize or avoid negative consequences.

When we communicate to children that the primary reason for reading is to earn a reward, we fail to impart reading's true value. Reading is its own reward and bestows immeasurable gifts. If we want to engage our students in reading over the summer, we must focus our efforts on the fundamental best practices that encourage children to read for a lifetime.

# Making the School's Books Available All Summer

While seeking out funding for book distribution programs, we cannot overlook the fact that we already have a lot of books kids could read over the summer—the books in our school libraries, classroom collections, and book rooms, which sit locked up inside our schools all summer. The key to our students' reading success—access to books—remains unavailable all summer while we allocate funding for summer school and year-round remediation programs. Why not open up the school and encourage every child to check out books for the summer?

One year, Donalyn looped with her fourth-grade students to fifth grade, which meant that she had more influence over summer reading because the children would be returning to her class. Right before the end of fourth grade, she talked with her students about the summer slide and encouraged all of them to check out at least four books for summer reading and take them home. One student, Sharille, spent every summer in the Dominican Republic with her grandparents, siblings, and cousins, while her parents remained in the United States to work extra jobs. Although the benefits of this annual trip were immeasurable from a personal and cultural standpoint, Donalyn knew Sharille wouldn't have access to many books in English unless she took books with her. Sharille loved the Dork Diary series by Rachel Renée Russell. Donalyn stuffed a bookbag full of as many books in the series as she could so Sharille would be able to take them with her for the summer. Expecting a 10-year-old to travel out of and back into the country with these books meant risking their loss, but making sure that Sharille had books she wanted to read made it a risk worth taking.

In August, Sharille walked back into Donalyn's class with every single book crammed into that well-traveled bookbag. She told Donalyn, "Mrs. Miller, it is so hot at my grandma's house. Whenever it got too hot for my cousins and me to play, we would all sit under the tree in our backyard, and we would all read Dork Diaries!" If she had lost every book, lending them to her still would have been worth it.

Yes, if we loan books over the summer, we are going to lose some. **But we would rather lose a book than lose a child. These are the stakes. We have to abdicate our role as book caretaker sometimes to remain committed to children.**

Colby's supervisor, Sue Haney, is principal of Parma Elementary School in Parma, Michigan, a small rural community without much access to books. Haney shares how her school provides children with ways to find and borrow books, and celebrate reading at school and home.

**Sue Haney**

# Our School Reading Community

*Our school reflects our belief that providing access to books and giving students choice is critical if we want our students to become avid, passionate, engaged readers.*

At our school, from the moment our students enter the parking lot, they have access to books in our Little Free Library that hangs from a pole right in front of the school. When students walk in the front doors, they find a table with free books they are welcome to take, where they can also leave books they are ready to give away. Inside my office, students can borrow books from a wall filled with bookshelves. As they walk down the hallways, they pass murals depicting favorite characters and covers from books we have read. In each classroom, students have access to libraries stocked with books. Yes, we have a school library, but it's important that this isn't the only place students have access to books or are encouraged to be readers. We are also aware many of our students do not have access to books at home, so throughout the year, we provide literacy events where families get free books to take home.

Our school reflects our belief that providing access to books and giving students choice is critical if we want our students to become avid, passionate, engaged readers. The changes we made to support reading are easy and doable—here's how you can start.

## LITTLE FREE LIBRARY

This was as simple as asking my father to build a Little Free Library for our school and stocking it with books. From that point on, it has become a revolving door for students to take or give a book. Every morning and every afternoon, I see students

opening the door to the Little Free Library to check out what new books are in there, as the selection is always changing. (You can find more information about Little Free Library programs, including blueprints for building libraries, at littlefreelibrary.org.)

### FREE-BOOK TABLE

As we bring new books in to keep our libraries current and fresh, we always have books we're ready to retire from our shelves. We place these gently used books on a table in our front hallway. As students walk by or wait for the morning bell to ring, they can check out the books on the table and take what they want. I often see teachers at this table, too, since a book that's no longer needed in one classroom may be just the book another teacher is looking for. They just have to beat the kids to the table!

### PRINCIPAL'S BOOKSHELF

I started a tradition of reading to my students every week in a morning assembly. As I read more and more books, my bookshelf began to grow, and students began stopping by my office to borrow the books I had read

or shared with them through read-alouds and book talks. I now have a wall of books for students to borrow. These days, at the beginning and the end of school, my office is flooded with students who want to learn more about the books we've read. They want to talk to me about a book we've read, to see what new books I may have, or to ask me to get a new book they've heard about.

I have often wondered about the excitement over my bookshelf, since the kids know our classrooms have libraries and our school library is well stocked. What I've come to realize is that often, it's more than a book they're after. There's something special about sharing books together, talking about what we thought of the books, and deciding on our next read. My check-out process for the books on my shelf is not the most sophisticated system, and it doesn't guarantee all the books will come back. Students simply write their names on a whiteboard beside the book they're borrowing. But as Donalyn Miller says, "I would rather lose a book than a reader." When students ask when they have to bring the book back, my answer is always the same: when you're finished reading it.

My time in front of that wall of books, talking to students about the books, and helping them select their next read, has become one of the best parts of my day. The connections I've made with students and the relationships we've built through these books will, I hope, be part of the reading memories my students carry with them from Parma Elementary.

## BOOK MURALS

Why not paint the walls? Who says the walls all have to be boring old white? It's important that our kids are inspired every day to be readers through our shared memories of our favorite books, author visits, and characters. We've painted pictures of books above lockers in our hallway so students are always reminded of the importance of literacy and reading at our school.

## CLASSROOM LIBRARIES

If we want our kids to read and become readers, we have to give them real, desirable access to books. Having a school library is not enough. Yes, our students go to the library, and the importance of a school library should never be underestimated. Our school library should be the center of our school, and going to the library should be an exciting time for our kids. But our kids sit in classrooms all day long, and they must have access to a variety of books there, too. If districts are not providing funds to each teacher every year to build a classroom library, they need to consider where the money is going—is it more important than providing books for readers?

## BOOKS IN HOMES

Many of our families do not have easy access to books. We not only need to help our families understand the importance of providing books at home, but also to help them acquire books. Every year, we have at least two book fairs and kick off each book fair with a family event on a Sunday afternoon. The Buy-One-Get-One fair enables families to buy one book and get another free. During the BOGO fair in the spring, our striving learners, with the help of our Title I teachers, select 10 to 12 books. The students take three to four of these books home when they leave in June; in July, we mail them three to four more books; and then in August, they get the rest of the books in the mail. Remember, these are high-interest books that they've selected, so getting this package in the mail is very exciting. This puts books in homes, and it promotes reading all summer long with books each child self-selected to read.

Along with providing books, we hold family literacy events throughout the year. When we have an author visit, we have a breakfast with the author where families can meet the author and get books signed. This generates excitement around a new book in their homes. We also host family breakfasts where our teachers emphasize the importance of reading with children at home, talk to families about how to read with their children, and share tools and strategies families can use. Every family in attendance gets at least one free book, and every child gets to select another book to take home.

It is our goal that every child at our school will create lasting reading memories that help them become engaged, passionate readers for the rest of their lives. We work hard to maintain a reading community and culture so anyone who attends or visits our school feels our energy and passion for reading.

## Closing Thoughts

Without ensuring that all kids have the book access they need, it is unlikely that we will ever close the widening gap between our most-advantaged and least-advantaged children. How can we build partnerships between schools, families, and our communities that provide each child a book flood?

**CHAPTER 2**

# School Libraries and Librarians: The Right of Every Child

See Donalyn and Colby discuss the importance of libraries and librarians at scholastic.com/GameChanger Resources

*"Libraries are a cornerstone of democracy—where information is free and equally available to everyone. People tend to take that for granted, and they don't realize what is at stake when that is put at risk."*

**—CARLA HAYDEN, LIBRARIAN OF CONGRESS**

As teachers and parents, we understand the role effective librarians play in connecting children with books, modeling and teaching literacy skills, and supporting instruction through library programs and curriculum support. Research proves children's access to a full-time, degreed librarian increases test scores, closes the achievement gap, and improves writing skills (Kachel & Lance, 2013).

Unfortunately, our librarian colleagues are under siege. Due to budget cuts in schools across the country and misunderstandings about the importance of school libraries, many school librarians are losing their jobs, finding themselves reassigned to jobs such as technology support specialists or elective teachers, or being forced to cover multiple schools on a rotating schedule. And many librarians who have managed to maintain full-time positions at one school have lost their library aides and experienced drastic cuts to book and supply budgets.

The defunding of school librarians should concern us all. When we consider the need for critical literacy skills, the need for information literacy, and the important role reading plays in building empathy for and understanding of the world, it's clear that we need our librarians more than ever. Cutting library positions and funding is shortsighted in light of our long-term goals to create an educated populace.

## Teaching Technology Skills vs. Literacy Skills

Our students, who do not remember a world without the Internet, are tech comfy, but not tech savvy. They need modeling and explicit instruction in how to use technology for academic, professional, and personal reasons. Librarians are best suited to do that job—supporting students and teachers in navigating social media, collaborating through online platforms, evaluating information for credibility and bias, and conducting research online. No matter what world our students inherit, they will need literacy skills. Yes, students need innovative learning opportunities, but those needs do not replace the ongoing need for a positive orientation toward reading and fundamental proficiency in literacy.

Many librarians worry that ensuring students' book access, matching children with books, and curating quality book collections are taking a backseat to other demands on their time. School librarians offer so much more to their communities than their book knowledge. We cannot disregard their importance in creating strong reading  communities and supporting reading instruction in a school. We must remember that librarians may be the only teachers in the school who have received formal training in book selection and current trends in children's and young adult literature. School librarians are integral to the development of reading cultures and irreplaceable when it comes to the reading development of children.

Bill Bass, a district administrator supervising technology and library programs in the St. Louis area, believes the role of librarians will evolve as new technologies and modalities change literacy, but supporting children's reading lives will remain constant. In his words:

> Libraries have long been spaces synonymous with reading and literacy, but I know that what it means to be literate in the digital age is vastly different than what it was in years past. Each day I see our kids interacting with a variety of different kinds of content and recognize that their reading lives are very different than mine was. School librarians are on the forefront of that work, with the library serving as a place of exploration and discovery beyond the classroom.
>
> Librarians are in the unique position to connect kids with books and other content in a variety of ways. Our cultural shift from print to digital texts may feel complicated, but ultimately, if we allow it, that shift can enhance our approach to reading instruction and provide appropriate, engaging texts to our kids. Regardless of the medium, one of the core tenets of library programs remains helping kids become lifelong readers.

## School Libraries vs. Classroom Libraries

Whenever we praise classroom libraries on social media, we hear from school librarians who feel that our comments may lead to reduced funding and support for school libraries and librarians. Let's be clear. Classroom libraries can never replace a school library collection curated and maintained by a certified librarian. Efforts to replace school libraries with satellite collections around the school are misguided and hinder students' academic progress. On the other hand, there is nothing sadder than a reading class without books for students to read. Providing young readers with continuous book access means offering books in classrooms, in school libraries, and at home. Funding and resources for classroom libraries should not supplant funding and resources for school libraries. Librarians, with their extensive knowledge in collection development and current trends in children's and young adult literature, should be an integral voice in conversations about classroom libraries. Territory wars that reduce or control book access don't benefit kids. It's not a competition—classroom libraries versus school libraries. Kids need books everywhere.

Jennifer LaGarde, former school librarian and national school librarian advocate, believes that classroom libraries provide school librarians with opportunities to support the reading development of students and the professional development of teachers. She envisions all adults in the school community working together to foster a love of reading and to model and teach the skills and attitudes children need to become lifelong readers.

---

**CHANGE IN ACTION**

**Jennifer LaGarde**

## Five Ways School Librarians Can Help Classroom Teachers Build Epic Classroom Libraries

*"I want our students to see the classroom library as the gateway to this room."*

Those were the words my principal used to inform ELA teachers at the middle school where I was the librarian of the district's plan to increase student access to books through an investment in classroom libraries. I'll never forget it.

With that sentence, she set three expectations for my classroom-teacher colleagues and me: 1) establish a common goal to help kids develop reading lives, 2) to do that, make sure they are surrounded by books, and 3) work together to make that happen.

I've thought about this moment many times over the years, especially when I've received questions from school librarians who feel threatened by district investments in classroom libraries. Too often, investment in classroom libraries strips funding from school libraries. While my district had eliminated funding for school libraries, my principal felt investing in our school library showed sustained commitment to the literacy needs of children. She always put the school's money where her mouth was. When I requested funding, or came to her with an idea for getting kids excited about reading, she always said yes.

In short, leadership matters. My principal's encouragement reassured me that support for classroom libraries was about book access for children and that she saw me as a leader in that work. While the absence of that type of leadership presents challenges for librarians who are already struggling to maintain adequate collections, it also presents important opportunities. Leadership, after all, is not a title; it's an action. When our districts throw support behind classroom libraries, we should be excited by the prospect of increasing students' book access, while also seizing on opportunities to present ourselves as literacy leaders. Here are five actions to consider.

## 1. TAKE INTEREST INVENTORIES

"Quality reading instruction does not begin with literature. It begins with students" (Crowder, 2017). I think about this reminder from middle school teacher Travis Crowder whenever I'm asked for a "list of books that every _____ should read." Just as there's no such thing as a "one-size-fits-all" bathing suit, there is no such thing as a list of books that's right for all readers. As teachers begin the journey of curating classroom library collections, help them keep the focus where it should be, on readers, by encouraging teachers to collect reading interest inventories. A quick Google search will yield numerous examples of inventories, and while that's a great place to start, I recommend working with teachers to create their own, focusing on the specific needs of their students. Keep in mind that students who have yet to develop reading lives may not have answers to questions such as, "What's your favorite book?" or "What genre do you like best?" I recommend asking questions that will provide you with good information, yet won't unintentionally diminish dormant readers, such as, "What do you like to do outside of school?" and "What was the last book you remember an adult reading to you? What did you like about it? What would have made it better?" Questions like those allow kids who haven't found "that" book yet to share their interests in and experiences with reading, without leaving them feeling inadequate. When we solicit students' experiences and interests and value them, we are more likely to create classroom libraries that reflect them.

## 2. EMBRACE INCLUSIVITY AND EQUITY

Every child deserves to see themselves, and their experiences, reflected in the books they read. But it's also important for them to see the experiences of others reflected in those books. Reading is not only the fundamental skill that underpins all learning, but also the key to developing empathy and compassion. School librarians should harness their knowledge of children's and young adult literature to help classroom teachers create an inclusive collection that celebrates the diversity of our global family and doesn't perpetuate stereotypes of marginalized groups.

I recommend leading teachers in the use of identity webs, such as those championed by Sara Ahmed and Harvey "Smokey" Daniels in their book *Upstanders* (Daniels & Ahmed, 2015). These simple but powerful tools will help you and your colleagues get to know students in a deep way. You can then use what you learn to create collections that empower kids to read about our global family. Social media movements and hashtags such as #weneeddiversebooks (also #WNDB) and #ownvoices are also great resources for connecting teachers to books made richer by authentic diverse voices. There is so much more to kids than what their demographic or testing data implies. As teachers get to know them in more meaningful ways, we can help them create classroom libraries worthy of their students.

### 3. ORGANIZE WITH STUDENTS IN MIND

The ways in which we organize our classroom or school libraries can determine the extent to which students develop rich reading lives. When we organize them by reading level, or we restrict student access to books based on those levels, we do several things: We make each student's reading level public, a practice that has been denounced by the American Library Association as an infringement on learner privacy (ALA, 2011). We shift focus from readers and their experiences with a text to the label they've been assigned. We associate reading with assessment in the minds of our students. We remove opportunities for them to select books in ways real readers do.

School librarians have an obligation to help classroom teachers organize their collections in ways that spark curiosity, generate high interest, promote diversity, and help students become independent library users. Their knowledge of children's and young adult literature is invaluable in creating collections. Classroom libraries should be spaces in which students spend very little time trying to find the right book and more time reading.

## 4. TAG TEAM BOOK TALKERS

What's the point of having a library stocked full of amazing books if no one wants to check them out? Getting kids excited about books is a time-tested librarian superpower, and one we can harness to help classroom teachers get the most from their collections. Donalyn Miller recommends using "preview stacks" as a way for kids to explore a number of books that the teacher selects for them, based on their knowledge of the child and of the books (Miller, 2013). It's a gentle way of saying, "Hey! We know you as a reader and here are some books we think you might love!" while providing students with the option of selecting books from the stack or from outside of it. School librarians can help teachers build preview stacks made up of titles from both the school and classroom collections.

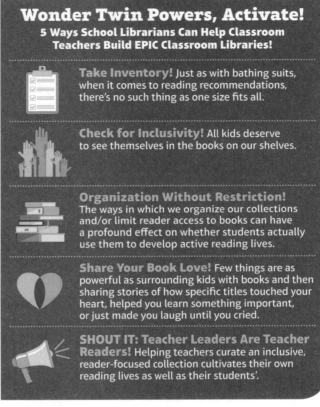

**Wonder Twin Powers, Activate!**
**5 Ways School Librarians Can Help Classroom Teachers Build EPIC Classroom Libraries!**

**Take Inventory!** Just as with bathing suits, when it comes to reading recommendations, there's no such thing as one size fits all.

**Check for Inclusivity!** All kids deserve to see themselves in the books on our shelves.

**Organization Without Restriction!** The ways in which we organize our collections and/or limit reader access to books can have a profound effect on whether students actually use them to develop active reading lives.

**Share Your Book Love!** Few things are as powerful as surrounding kids with books and then sharing stories of how specific titles touched your heart, helped you learn something important, or just made you laugh until you cried.

**SHOUT IT: Teacher Leaders Are Teacher Readers!** Helping teachers curate an inclusive, reader-focused collection cultivates their own reading lives as well as their students'.

(Courtesy of Jennifer LaGarde)

Passion is contagious, and it's important for us to share our passion for books through book talks. Few practices are as powerful as surrounding children with books and sharing stories of how specific ones touched your heart, or taught you something important, or just made you laugh until you cried. School librarians, as experienced book talkers, should not only model this practice for teachers (who may not have a lot of experience doing it), but also build a partnership with teachers so they can support and encourage students with their passion for reading! Some of my most rewarding experiences as a school librarian involved book talking a stack with a teacher, in front of kids who were delighted to hear us banter back and forth about books and how they made us feel as readers.

Plus, by working together, we doubled our book-talking firepower for kids, reminding them that we were both there to help them find a great book and, perhaps, to talk about a book we were reading or had recently finished. Despite the stereotype of reading as a solitary activity—of a person curled up in an easy chair, engrossed in a book—it can be an inherently social activity. The first thing we want to do when we read a book that moves us is to share it with someone else. Talking about books builds a connection between our students and us.

## 5. ACKNOWLEDGE THE IMPORTANCE OF TEACHERS AS READERS

Curating a reader-focused collection is especially challenging for teachers who do not read many books in their own lives. There are so many ways to get teachers reading. Start a teacher book club, use social media to help teachers talk about books, work alongside them to create book trailers, host a #30secondbooktalk challenge so teachers can compete for the title of best book talker, or create "What I'm Reading" signs for them to put outside their classroom doors. There are countless ways for you to cultivate teachers' reading lives. We would never hire a music teacher who didn't love music. So why would we allow a classroom teacher who is charged with helping kids grow into readers opt out of being a reader? Just like school libraries, classroom libraries can be invaluable resources in helping to create a schoolwide culture in which reading is more than a skill to be mastered.

I understand the urge to question classroom libraries while so many school libraries are neglected and underfunded. But in the end, if our goal is to democratize information for all learners, while helping them develop empowered lives, we should celebrate any initiative that puts books in the hands of children. After all, our jobs are not about books. They are about readers.

# Closing Thoughts

Every child deserves to attend school with a library and degreed school librarian. Students without access to school librarians and well-funded libraries are at an academic disadvantage and miss out on building a relationship with a knowledgeable reading mentor. Advocate for your librarians and libraries and work with your community to build an understanding of why libraries still matter.

See Donalyn
and Colby
discuss the
importance
of classroom
libraries at
scholastic.com/
GameChanger
Resources

**CHAPTER 3**

# Classroom Libraries: A Living, Breathing Reading Community

*"Reading should not be presented to children as a chore or duty.
It should be offered to them as a precious gift."*

**—KATE DICAMILLO**

In addition to school library access, children benefit from classroom libraries. They read 50 to 60 percent more in classrooms with adequate libraries than in classrooms without them (Allington, 2012; Morrow, 2006; Neuman, 1999). Findings from the 2005 National Assessment for Educational Progress Report (Kelley & Clausen-Grace, 2009) reveal that children with well-designed classroom libraries spend more time reading, interact more with books, show more positive attitudes about reading, and attain higher levels of reading achievement. According to the National Council of Teachers of English Position Statement on Classroom Libraries (2017), in partnership with school libraries, "Classroom libraries—physical or virtual—play a key role in providing access to books and promoting literacy; they have the potential to increase student motivation, engagement, and achievement and help students become critical thinkers, analytical readers, and informed citizens."

Ensuring that all children have the books they need is more than an access issue—it's an equity issue. Children's book access should not exist at the whim of administrative support. In school districts where the benefits of classroom libraries remain unrecognized or funding priorities don't include books, there is little institutional support for developing and sustaining classroom libraries. Too often, teachers (and many librarians) subsidize their schools' budgets by buying books with their own money, which is particularly difficult for new teachers. All teachers, new and experienced alike, struggle to build and manage classroom libraries in response to students' ever-changing interests and needs.

In our survey of 8,506 kindergarten through 12th-grade teachers, 83 percent reported that zero to 25 percent of the funding for their classroom libraries came from their school or district budgets. Only five percent reported that their classroom libraries are fully funded by their schools. Teachers cobble together money and books for their classrooms through grants, personal funds, book sales, and donations (Miller & Sharp, 2018).

Annie Ward and Maggie Hoddinott, district literacy leaders from Mamaroneck Union Free School District in New York, have developed clear channels between district administration and classroom teachers to provide children with "on-demand" book access in response to students' needs and interests.

**CHANGE IN ACTION**

**Annie Ward and Maggie Hoddinott**

## Riverkeepers: High-Leverage Strategies to Keep Vital Streams of Books Flowing

Third-grade teacher Liz Johnson puts a copy of *Dog Man: A Tale of Two Kitties* into Gabriel's hands just in time for Memorial Day weekend. Gabriel has been on the move since the original *Dog Man* unleashed a stream of voluminous reading, and Liz recognizes the need to maintain his momentum. The timely delivery of Gabriel's next-up book is the final link in a chain of deliberate actions taken by committed educators at every level of the organization. Just as riverkeepers protect precious waterways, effective school and district leaders make it their mission to keep steady streams of compelling books flowing continuously into every classroom by…

## GENEROUSLY BUDGETING CLASSROOM LIBRARIES

- Riverkeeper leaders know the research on the benefits of voluminous, engaged reading. They cite it persuasively and advocate to establish and maintain robust book budgets for their districts and schools.
- These leaders monitor spending carefully and ensure that every penny earmarked for books is spent on books. They hold funds sacred and fend off requests for unprioritized materials.

## ALLOCATING MONEY FOR BOOKS, GLORIOUS BOOKS!

- Riverkeeper leaders know that readers thrive on a diet of authentic literature of all kinds. They make sure that the entire budget is spent on real, irresistible texts—NOT on dollar-sucking programs or controlled texts.
- These leaders provide librarians and ELA teachers with steady annual allocations. Any dry spell in the flow of book money devastates school and classroom libraries and plunges readers into book deserts.
- Riverkeeper leaders distribute responsibility for book ordering. In Mamaroneck, for example, we budget as follows:
  - A substantial allocation directly to librarians and teachers at three points during the year in order for them to "build libraries for the children they expect and customize collections for the children they meet"
  - An allocation for school administrators to apply to building-specific priorities
  - An allocation at the district level administered by the literacy ambassador to ensure consistency and currency across collections

## STREAMLINING AND DEMYSTIFYING THE ORDERING PROCESS

- Riverkeeper leaders work closely with business offices to understand the steps necessary to order specific titles rather than prepackaged collections of books.
- These leaders demystify ordering procedures for teachers: They explain how to procure hand-selected books. Knowing that additional monies sometimes become available with short turnaround time as the year unfolds, leaders encourage teachers to keep wish lists.

- Riverkeeper leaders identify passionate, knowledgeable book mavens and provide opportunities for them to support teachers in knowing and ordering the latest and greatest titles as well as books for children with niche interests.
- They familiarize teachers with reliable sources of new titles and include book-talking rituals at faculty and grade-level team meetings.

### TRACKING SPENDING AND FOLLOWING UP

- Riverkeeper leaders audit teachers' purchases to track spending patterns. They highlight teachers who have purchased books with specific children in mind and follow up with teachers who have not spent their allocations. When book flows ebb, collections stagnate and kids suffer!
- Riverkeeper leaders look downstream daily. They peruse classroom libraries; they confer with children about what they're reading; they look in book boxes and backpacks. When classroom libraries are not vibrant and children are not reading voluminously, leaders identify and remove the obstacles that block flow (e.g., unreliable allocations, confusion with ordering procedures).

### WEEDING ROUTINELY

- Just as rivers need to be dredged, books must be weeded out to make way for appealing new arrivals. Riverkeeper leaders encourage healthy turnover by ensuring books flow reliably into classroom libraries, clarifying weeding criteria and procedures, and providing time for teachers to discard MUSTIE books (books that are Misleading, Ugly, Superceded, Trivial, Irrelevant, and may be obtained Elsewhere; developed by the Texas State Library and Archives Commission).

Protecting and curating the flow of books into classrooms and kids' hands is an ongoing, vital responsibility. Even as they track every penny, riverkeeper leaders internalize Donalyn's admonition that "It's better to lose a book than to lose a child." Whether a lost book is gathering dust under someone's bed or has become a dog-eared favorite, riverkeeper leaders channel Elsa and "let it go," budgeting for its replacement. They know it is penny wise and pound foolish to impose penalties for lost books or to curb children's borrowing privileges. Incidentally, Gabriel devoured *A Tale of Two Kitties* over the long weekend, and Liz cheerfully reported it was the second copy she had purchased for her class, using her allocation to fuel its viral popularity.

If invested and informed administrators like Annie and Maggie gave you money for a classroom library, what would you ask for? What does a "well-designed" and "adequate" classroom library look like to you? How can you determine if a classroom library meets the minimum literacy needs of the children in that classroom? Imagine you are on a team evaluating the classroom libraries at a school. What criteria would you use?

While any classroom library must be customized according to the academic and personal needs of the readers it serves, there are some general considerations when creating one. Based on best-practices research and our experience as teachers, we suggest evaluating your classroom library according to these four categories:

- **Quantity:** How many books are in the library? How many children have daily access to the library? Do you have enough books per child to offer variety?

- **Diversity:** Does the library offer a wide range of text levels, genres, topics, and perspectives? Can young readers find books reflecting their experiences? Can they find books they can read with some ease and some challenge?

- **Currency:** Does the library reflect current trends in children's and young adult literature? Does the library contain information from credible, current sources? Is it in good physical condition? Does it represent modern thinking and experiences from global perspectives?

- **Organization:** Is the library easy for children to use without a teacher? Is there a system for checking out/in books? Are the books organized in appealing ways that invite students to browse them?

## Quantity

Classroom libraries filled with many books offer children variety and ensure they can find something they can read and are interested in reading. Experts and professional organizations vary on how many books classroom libraries should contain. The American Library Association (Hack, Hepler, & Hickman, 1993) recommends 300 titles, including single and multiple copies, in the permanent collection, with rotating supplemental titles from the school library. The International Literacy Association (formerly the International Reading Association) advises seven books per student,

and for school library collections 20 books per student (IRA, 2000). Literacy thought leaders Irene Fountas and Gay Su Pinnell recommend 500 to 800 books total (2018). Richard Allington, author and researcher, suggests in order to meet the wide range of reading abilities and interests in a typical classroom, classroom libraries should include 1,000 books with at least 500 unique titles (Allington, et al., 1996). Based on this range, classroom libraries should include a minimum of 300 titles and up to 1,000 books or more.

In 2013, Scholastic surveyed 3,800 classroom teachers and asked how many books they had in their classroom libraries. Less than 40 percent had the minimum recommended number of books: 300 (Scholastic, 2013). Of course, creating a classroom library that serves all students requires more than just putting books on the shelves. It's better to have a smaller library with books children want to read than a larger one filled with uninteresting books. Don't fill the shelves for the sake of filling them!

## Diversity

When assembling book collections and book lists for children, educators (and caregivers) must consider diversity in all the ways young readers need. **Children become stronger readers and thinkers when they read widely in a range of genres, at a range of levels, and on a range of topics, and when they are exposed to a range of formats and voices.** Researchers following trends in the results of the National Assessment of Educational Progress (NAEP) since 1990 have found that fourth graders' reading achievement increases as the diversity of their reading experiences increases (USDE, 2017).

To ensure that all children can find accessible books to read, classroom libraries must include books at text levels at least two years below grade level and at least two years above grade level (Allington & Gabriel, 2012). Depending on where your students are in any given year, the range may widen in either direction. Be sure the books in your library reflect the range of readers in your classroom. When we put books on the shelves without consideration of the children in the room, we create de facto book deserts for some readers (Harvey & Ward, 2017).

Offering books in a variety of formats—picture books, graphic novels, ebooks, audiobooks, and so forth—gives students more options for connecting with reading. Series fiction, graphic novels, and magazines in particular lead many young people to lifelong reading (Krashen, 2004). Learning to read different genres and formats increases young readers' skill and interest in reading (Miller & Kelley, 2013).

Above all, diverse collections include books that capture a range of people's ethnicities, cultures, races, abilities, genders, and sexual identities. Books written from a variety of perspectives and in a variety of voices foster empathy and affirm the history, culture, family background, and experiences of every child. We live in a wide world populated by many different kinds of people, and the books we promote and share with children must reflect that truth.

## Currency

Keeping a book collection current doesn't mean you need to buy every book in the new, hot series. A third-grade classroom library doesn't need every Rainbow Fairies or Geronimo Stilton book to give children what they need. However, a collection built solely from garage sale purchases and the books your own children have outgrown isn't ideal. No matter how you acquire new books for your classroom, school, or home libraries, those books must be engaging books for children. Weed out books that are in bad condition or no longer meet the needs of your students.

Regularly, examine books for damage, yellowing, and general physical condition and appeal. While we have both been known to tape a book back together so it makes it to the end of the school year, books that are falling apart should be replaced as quickly as possible, as funds allow. Even evergreen favorites like *Where the Red Fern Grows* and *Bud, Not Buddy* should be replaced when updated editions are released so students can enjoy the new covers and benefit from any updated material.

Nonfiction titles should contain the most accurate, up-to-date information we can provide. From time-to-time, check the copyright dates on your nonfiction books and replace or remove any out-of-date titles. Books about popular culture, celebrity biographies, and "Best of…" anthologies age quickly as children's tastes change. As human innovation and experience advance, we need to update books about history, science, and art, too. If your book on Presidents of the United States lists George W. Bush as our current Commander-in-Chief, you need a new book!

Be mindful that some books we remember lovingly from childhood are culturally tone deaf now and perpetuate stereotypes that negatively portray or marginalize groups of people. Revered "classics" such as *Little House on the Prairie* and *Doctor Dolittle*, for example, portray racist, colonial stereotypes about indigenous and African people. We don't feel every problematic book should be eliminated. We feel they should be read and discussed so children come to understand how the books we read can break down stereotypes or reinforce them. However, problematic books should not be children's sole exposures to different cultures. **Children deserve positive, affirming portrayals of as many cultures and experiences as possible, and they need the skills to read critically for agenda, bias, prejudice, and point of view** (Lifshitz, 2017).

## Organization

Both of us are low-frills, no-fuss teachers when it comes to organizing our classrooms and classroom libraries—foregoing decorations in favor of ease of use, durability, and spaces for students' interests and ideas. To our minds, book bins labeled with colored duct tape work just as well as expensive templates from an online store, and the money saved can be used for purchasing more books. We admire educators who can pull off a clever classroom design that works efficiently!

When setting up our classroom libraries, we create systems that help students locate, check out, and return books, require as little day-to-day maintenance as possible, take up just the right amount of space in our classrooms, and support the reading communities we are striving to build.

Donalyn has tried numerous systems for checking in and checking out classroom library books, and she has learned that the best system is one she can maintain over the school year and involves students as much as possible. After trying everything from boxes stuffed with students' checkout cards to cloud-based databases, she realized that the simplest and most effective checkout system used to best advantage the resources and real-world conditions in her classroom. At the

*Game Changer! Book Access for All Kids*

end of every class, Donalyn parked a student at her classroom doorway to ask their classmates if they checked out any books that day. Those students who did check out a book would use an iPad to photograph themselves holding the book. Those "shelfies" (selfies with books) remained on the photo roll of the iPad until the book was returned. Not only did Donalyn and her students have a better understanding of what books were checked out, they had a visual record of books that students self-selected—an ongoing celebration of their reading lives and the books that mattered to them.

As Colby describes in the following reflection about reorganizing his classroom library, selecting books and organizing the library space involves learning about and responding to the reading interests and needs of individual students and considering how the library is used from the first day of school to the last.

# Colby's Classroom Library

It was the end of a school day in late May, and I stood in the middle of my third-grade classroom, surrounded by books. As I was glancing at the fantasy section of my classroom library, Deborah Freedman's *Shy* caught my eye and reminded me of the previous winter when my student Alan read that book for the first time. Alan started the school year thinking he hated reading, until he read *Shy*, the first book I remember him falling in love with. He fell in love with many more. Then I walked over to the graphic novel section and grabbed the first book in Kazu Kibuishi's Amulet series. Every year, more than half my class would read the entire series. Replacing beat-up, well-loved copies was becoming an annual summer tradition.

## A New Grade... and a New Classroom Library

Earlier that day I had learned that I would be switching from teaching third grade to teaching fifth grade. My heart sank thinking about the grade-level colleagues with whom I'd no longer be working, Mrs. Woolworth and Mrs. Powers. And then, I started to worry about transitioning to a fifth-grade classroom library. I wondered: Do fifth graders read Amulet? Probably, but what else do they read? I had taught fourth grade four years earlier, but a lot can happen in four years in the children's publishing industry. Thousands of middle-grade novels had been published since then, and I'd given away many of the books from my fourth-grade classroom library to students and other teachers.

I spent the next two weeks checking out social media to see what fourth- and fifth-grade teachers' students were reading. I listened to episodes of fifth-grade teacher Corrina Allen's "Books Between" podcast, and studied fourth-grade teacher Stacey Riedmiller's Instagram feed. I marveled at how much readers grew in just a couple of years. The thought of transitioning to a fifth-grade classroom library was both exciting and terrifying.

As we inched closer to the end of the school year, I spent each day going through baskets in my classroom library, touching each of the 3,000+ books and deciding on the ones I would take with me to fifth grade, and the ones I would give to Mrs. Woolworth, Mrs. Powers, and my third-grade students. Tough decisions had to be made: Do I need every book in the Judy Moody series? Do fifth graders read Babymouse? What in the world do fifth graders read for nonfiction? The process was taking FOREVER. I came to the realization that if I stressed out over each and every book, I wouldn't get through the entire collection before August, and I could kiss my summer vacation goodbye. So I turned it up a notch. I gave away nearly 500 books to teachers, our school's Little Free Library, and my students. Around 2,500 books made the journey down the hall to my fifth-grade classroom.

## Fellow Readers to the Rescue!

When summer vacation started, I tweeted my Nerdy Book Club friends for advice on what books I should read over the summer to prepare for my move to fifth grade. I was flooded with responses, which helped me assemble and organize my summer reading pile. I read many books that I had missed over the years because I was teaching younger students—books such as Rob Buyea's *Because of Mr. Terupt*, Suzanne Collins's *Gregor the Overlander*, and *Esperanza Rising* by Pam Muñoz Ryan.

I spent the summer reading as many middle-grade novels as I could. At conferences, I talked to teachers and librarians about books I should add to my classroom library. While at a Scholastic Reading Summit, I stocked up on Raina

Telgemeier graphic novels, Kwame Alexander novels in verse, and anything else my educator friends told me to buy.

As summer came to a close, I was feeling pretty good about my fifth-grade classroom library, knowing that it, **like any classroom library, must be treated like a living, breathing organism. It needs constant care (organizing, weeding, cleaning). It must be fed (brand-new books, replacement books, gap-fillers). And it needs space (new shelves, new tubs, more displays).**

## Rolling Up Our Sleeves

A couple of weeks before the first day of school, I went to my classroom to begin setting it up. Although the room was filled with moving boxes, old textbooks, and random electrical wires that had to be dealt with, all I wanted to do was work on my classroom library. The library is the heart of so much of what we do, so I wanted to make sure I gave it the love and care it deserved. Nonetheless, I promised myself that I wouldn't work on it until the rest of my room was done. That promise lasted 15 minutes. My library was where my heart was.

My classroom library books are sorted by genre, author, and topic (Donalyn's classroom library, too), and each of those sections is numbered. I put a small round sticker on the cover of each book and write the book's section number on it. This allows my students to easily return books to their designated sections.

I was lucky enough to have my friend, retired school librarian Margie Culver, help me. She put hundreds of stickers on covers, and then she began sorting the books based on where they would go in the library. We discovered that the organization of the nonfiction section needed some work. The topics were very general: biography, social studies, science, and history. Margie used her expertise to help me think about how to make the topics more specific, which would in turn help my students find books. The library now contains sections labeled "Biographies of Artists," "Dinosaurs," and "World War I."

The books in my classroom library are placed in tubs designed to hold shoes and cost around a dollar each. The label on the front of each tub includes the titles of the books that go in it, and the number corresponding to that group of books. In the past, those labels would often fall off. It was quite annoying. Moving to a new grade level gave me the excuse to try something new. I went with duct tape because it's sturdy, easy to write on, and super sticky.

I love the beautiful labels some teachers create for their baskets, but I'm more of a functional-labels type of teacher. I wanted students to be able to quickly identify the nonfiction tubs and the fiction tubs, so I went with yellow tape for nonfiction and blue tape for fiction. Some of the tubs (graphic novels, poetry, etc.) include both fiction and nonfiction texts. For them, I went with green tape (yellow + blue = green). Margie did so much to help me organize the nonfiction section of the library, creating all of the labels. I couldn't have done it without her. Classroom teachers can learn so much from working alongside school librarians.

Once all the books were in tubs, and all the tubs were on bookshelves, I started to see the holes in the library. We were missing two books in the Amulet series. The World War I section had very few books, while the World War II section had many. I used a little money I had set aside to purchase missing series books, round out nonfiction tubs that were sparse, and order a couple of Kate DiCamillo books to fill up her tub. You can never have enough Kate DiCamillo books.

In the days leading up to the first day of school, I must have moved the bookshelves around five or six times, knowing I wouldn't have a good feeling for where they should go until the kids arrived in class. But that didn't stop me from overanalyzing the library layout.

## Open for Business

The first few days of school were filled with book magic. Children I had in third grade were eager to show their new classmates books they had loved two years earlier. All the kids were drawn to authors who they had read the previous year, such as Christopher Paul Curtis, Gary Paulsen, and Jennifer L. Holm. The graphic novel section quickly became a huge mess, with books flying all over the place. Our classroom library was helping us build a reading community.

After the first week of school, I moved a couple of bookshelves to allow more space for the high-traffic sections (graphic novels, fantasy novels, books by specific authors). I replaced a couple of rickety old shelves with a giant two-sided bookshelf that the school librarian no longer needed. All in all, it took about three months before the library started feeling right.

My school district gives each classroom teacher $250 a year to spend on their classroom library. It isn't much, but I know it is more than a lot of teachers get. I could have easily spent it at the start of the school year, but I wanted to get to know my students.

The first few months in the fifth grade were fascinating. Children who were obsessed with Kate DiCamillo and Roald Dahl in third grade were now obsessed with Suzanne Collins and Jacqueline Woodson. One constant—their obsession with series. In third grade it was Babymouse and Lunch Lady. Wings of Fire and Land of Stories captivated my fifth graders. I waited until January to spend my $250. By that time, I had learned the nonfiction topics my students wanted more of, what series books I needed extra copies of, and what new series might be a good fit for my readers.

During the first 100 days, I made five major tweaks to my classroom library.

**Completed series.** My students were loving the Last Kids on Earth series and Land of Stories series. So I made sure we had multiple copies of the first couple of books in those series, and at least one copy of later books.

**Purchased additional copies of popular books.**

**Acquired a series that was new to me.** A handful of my students were devouring the Wings of Fire series. One of them borrowed it from her older sister, and the love for those books spread like wildfire.

**Stocked up on sequels to read-alouds.** Our second read-aloud of the year was Jason Reynolds's *Ghost*, which ended on a bit of a cliffhanger. My students were dying to read the second book, *Patina*. The one copy we had in our classroom library was not going to cut it, so I purchased a couple more.

**Added audiobooks.** We have a class Audible account that my students use to download audiobooks, which they listen to as they follow along in physical copies of the books. Many of my students find that doing this helps them access books they are dying to read but that might be a little hard to comprehend reading the text alone.

As the school year was coming to a close, I realized my classroom library had grown throughout the year, right alongside my readers. More than 500 books had been weeded out. Some of the books that I thought my students were going to love had received little or no interest. We can't romanticize books in our classroom library. The books we choose must be the books our students will read. During the year, I added hundreds of books for a variety of reasons: my students requested them, they related to titles and topics students were enjoying, and they were newly published titles fitting my students' reading interests.

My classroom library will never be complete. New readers will come each year with new interests. Books that were a favorite one year will collect dust a couple of years later. My job as a reading teacher is to make sure that my students have an opportunity to fall in love with reading, and one of the best ways to support them is developing a classroom library that evolves to meet students' interests and needs.

# Closing Thoughts

Classroom libraries are important resources for teachers and students and should be fully supported with funding and professional development. Classroom libraries invite kids into a world of reading and provide in-the-moment support for students' reading lives and your classroom instruction. Teachers never finish building our classroom libraries, because these spaces change and evolve in response to the young readers in our classrooms from year to year. We cannot imagine teaching reading in a classroom without a library in it.

# Books of Their Own: The Power of Book Ownership

*"Books make great gifts because they have whole worlds inside of them."*
— **NEIL GAIMAN**

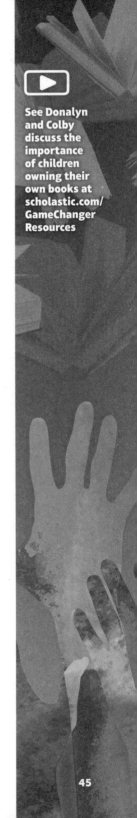

See Donalyn and Colby discuss the importance of children owning their own books at scholastic.com/ GameChanger Resources

A National Trust survey of more than 18,000 young people from ages 8 to 17 identified a strong connection between students' book ownership and their reading ability and motivation. Unlike their peers who do not own many books, children with sufficient book ownership live in homes with books, are more likely to receive books as presents, read more often and for longer time periods, express higher engagement and interest in reading, read more widely and in higher volume, find it easier to locate interesting books, and achieve higher levels of education attainment (Clark & Poulton, 2011). **Ensuring all children own at least a few books must be a priority if we're to provide equitable book access.**

Book ownership is also an important factor in a child's reading identity development. Children who own books are more likely to take personal ownership of their reading lives. When children have books at home, they possess on-demand access to those books, which they can read whenever they have a free moment— a key to home-reading momentum. Children are more likely to own books matching their individual reading preferences. While teachers and librarians strive to build collections, book lists, and text sets that appeal to a wide range of readers, children and their caregivers can select books with individual and family needs and interests in mind. Home book collections provide young readers with customized access to books chosen just for them.

Donalyn offers the following suggestions for supporting families' book ownership.

- **Provide families with a student-created list of book recommendations.** Several times a year, Donalyn shared a Google sheet with families listing her fifth- and sixth-grade students' book-talk recommendations. When students gave book talks, a classmate entered the title, author (and illustrator), and genre of each recommended title into the Google sheet. The filled-in sheets provided a record of the authentic reading experiences and preferences of the children in Donalyn's classes from year to year. Peer recommendations hold more sway with kids than recommendations by adults—no matter how informed those adults may be about children's and young adult literature. After all, every book on the students' list was kid-tested and approved!

- **Share with families high-quality sources for book recommendations,** such as A Mighty Girl (amightygirl.com) and Social Justice Books (socialjusticebooks.org/booklists). Look for sources emphasizing readers' interests as book-selection criteria, not reading levels or curriculum connections. Seek out sources recommending a wide variety of books from different perspectives and experiences.

- **Promote public library literacy events and library sales.** Partner with your youth services librarians to provide information about upcoming programs and family events such as author visits, summer reading programs, and book drives. Many public libraries hold scheduled book sales of library discards, duplicates, and donations, and/or have an ongoing book sale during regular operating hours.

- **Host book fairs and book sales at school.** Without brick-and-mortar bookstores, many communities lack direct access to new books for children. We cannot assume that families have the ability to purchase books online or can afford new hardcover books. Bringing pop-up book shopping events into your school, such as book fairs and book sales, gives families (and educators) the opportunity to shop for low-cost new books, while receiving advice from teachers and librarians in selecting books for their children.

- **Give away books at family events.** Reinforce the importance of reading to your school community and support your students' book ownership by giving away books at all family events—not just literacy events.

- **Apply for grants or solicit community funding for book donation programs.** Reading Is Fundamental, one of the largest nonprofit organizations providing books to low-income families, offers Books for Ownership grants to schools and community organizations. Talk with representatives at your local small business organization or Chamber of Commerce about the importance of book ownership in your community and solicit their support. Create a Google sheet of grant sources and encourage colleagues to add to it as they discover new ones.

- **Create and stock Little Free Libraries, book baskets, or take-a-book stations wherever families with kids might gather.** Investigate opportunities to provide families with books by visiting apartment complexes, laundromats, daycare centers, and doctors' offices. Where are the book deserts in your communities? How can you increase physical access to books in them? Determine ahead of time how and when you will refresh the books, or sign up school or community volunteers to sponsor a location for book distribution and check it periodically to make sure it's clean and well stocked.

While book swaps and book drives are important initiatives, they tend to redistribute books from families that have many books to families that don't. When the only books children own are someone else's discards and hand-me-downs, it can affect their self-esteem and their perception about books and reading. So consider initiatives that provide children with new books whenever possible. Even one or two a year can make a big difference. Every child should own at least a few, new self-selected books.

Brigid Hubberman, founder of Children's Reading Connection, a national literacy organization working to support literacy efforts in communities, offers additional suggestions for lifting up children and families through book gifts and celebrations.

**CHANGE IN ACTION**

**Brigid Hubberman**

## Belong With Books

*The gift of books builds bridges between families, schools, and community.*

Four-year-old Xuan Kim was new—new to the country, new to the culture, and new to the community, as was his family. As if navigating all of that wasn't enough for a young Vietnamese child who had been in the United States for four weeks, he was leaving his family for the first time and going off to pre-kindergarten where all of the words surrounding him—spoken and written—were completely new. As Xuan Kim boarded the bus, his family felt some of the same anxiety he did.

Then one day Xuan Kim's teacher presented each of her students with a special gift, a copy of *The Bus for Us* by Suzanne Bloom. He couldn't believe it was his to take home—that the book was his to keep always.

The gift of that beautiful book, coming at that important time in his life, meant so much to Xuan Kim. It gave him pride of ownership, especially since there were few things he could call his very own. What is more, he felt a special new connection to his pre-kindergarten classmates through their shared book experience. He felt a new and warm sense of belonging.

The book also carried another wonder. Imagine Xuan Kim's surprise and delight to find the story's words in Vietnamese, alongside those in English. His reaction to seeing his family's home language, "his" words, in such an unfamiliar world, was to hug the book. Realizing that his copy of the book had been personalized with his name on a label made him feel known and valued.

Xuan Kim continued to turn the pages and delighted at the simple and comfortably predictable story featuring children waiting for the school bus. He smiled when he realized each page depicted a new vehicle. He paused to touch the page on which he noticed there was a little boy who looked a lot like him, waiting for the bus.

Xuan Kim's copy of *The Bus for Us* was his welcome into school and into a community of book owners and readers, giving him a new way of participating in the world. It was also a beautiful bridge connecting every child who read the book, for learning to read and loving reading.

Xuan Kim rushed home that day excited to show his family his beautiful new book, and he couldn't wait for his family to read it to him. His father described feeling deeply touched and honored by the gift bridging their cherished old world and exciting new world with a story in both languages. He went to the school the next day for the first time to thank the teacher, and he let her know how many times they had already read *The Bus for Us* together and how much it meant to Xuan Kim and his whole family.

Xuan Kim was one of 1,200 new pre-kindergartners from New York's Ithaca City School District Pre-K and Tompkins Community Action Head Start who received *The Bus for Us* as a gift, with funding made possible by Ithaca's Alternatives Federal Credit Union. The book has helped to build community, strengthen families, enhance school environments, and enrich children's pathways to reading in a wondrous way by sending the clear message that all children and their families belong.

Books that children can call their own ensure everyday access. Each time they open those books and soak in the story, it is with new meaning, new mastery, and new affection. Those books also can become a form of cultural capital—an investment in the idea that every child and family is a participant in community life, not just a spectator.

It is essential that we place as many books as possible into the hands, homes, and hearts of our children, and that we do all we can to support families in making the wonder of words and the joy of books part of everyday life. A future filled with hope and promise begins with books at home. Together we can make that vision a reality!

Make it count. Here's how to give books to children in ways that build bridges between families, schools, and communities:

- Gift books in as many ways as you can to create a culture of literacy. Give a book to new babies at birth as a gift from the community, and welcome children to school with a book. Give books at the holidays and on special occasions, and create events bringing everyone together to elevate and celebrate best-loved books.
- Choose a book of the highest quality—one that depicts children from all kinds of families and captures experiences that are meaningful. Make sure that children can see themselves in the book's illustrations.
- Personalize the book for each child with a name label and perhaps even a personal inscription such as, "I believe in you."
- Make sure the book is presented as a true gift from someone in the child's life.
- Build excitement and anticipation around book gifts and create traditions for your students and their families. Children will then associate other books with the same joy, wonder, and love.

# Closing Thoughts

Book ownership influences children's reading identities and their feelings about reading. Children read more and express more enthusiasm for reading when they own books. How can we guarantee that every child in our communities owns at least a few books?

See Donalyn and Colby discuss text leveling systems at scholastic.com/ GameChanger Resources

# On the Level: Some Truths About Text Leveling Systems

*"Kids shouldn't be told that they can't read a good book just because it isn't in their level. It's just not fair."*

**—JAKE, FOURTH GRADER**

There are few topics more polarizing in literacy education than the role of leveling in matching children with books to read. In rigid conditions, which limit children's reading choices to books "at their level" and emphasize reading level measures as the most important marker of children's reading development, many children never develop personal reasons for reading or the skills needed to self-select books. Readers need abundant opportunities to examine and evaluate books—selecting books for their own interests and purposes, sampling different formats, genres, voices, and writing styles, finding authors who resonate with them, and challenging themselves to read widely. As adult readers, freed from outside control of our reading choices, we can confidently navigate a bookstore or library to find books we want to read. If we envision our children as lifelong readers, they must learn how to choose books for themselves. When we rely too much on leveling systems for matching young readers with books, we deny them valuable opportunities to fine-tune their book selection skills under our guidance.

On the other hand, turning children loose in the library and encouraging them to pick "a just right book" isn't enough support. When a child self-selects a book she cannot read, it is doubtful that much reading engagement or growth will occur. Overwhelmed by the sheer number of books published for children each year, even the most knowledgeable teacher or librarian can struggle with providing individualized book recommendations for a large group of students. Many educators and caregivers depend on reading level information to narrow available books for children to more accessible options. Leveling systems give adults an easy (if incomplete and inadequate) way to measure and communicate reading progress. Leveling becomes a shortcut, but it isn't a substitute for knowing books and knowing our students as readers.

# How Levels Can Limit Reading Engagement

Current educational practices have bought into leveling as a measure of reading growth. In many schools, educators must track and report children's reading levels several times a year. (We have even seen teachers requiring students to track their reading level progress on public charts displayed on the wall!) Teachers use leveling measurements to identify children who are not "making progress" and to share reading level information with caregivers. Educators use reading level measurements to group children and decide which children require intervention and support services. Discussions about who is "on level" and who isn't drive instructional decision-making and resource allocation in many schools.

Instead of free and open access to books in school libraries, students in many schools must select books from a specific reading level or point level range. Such restrictions can often warp students' orientation toward reading and how they see themselves as readers.

During a visit to an elementary school in the Midwest, Donalyn witnessed firsthand the negative consequences of this slavish devotion to leveling. While she was in the library, a group of third graders came in to return and check out books. The children wore index cards clipped to their shirts. On one side of the card was the child's name. On the back were layers of sticky labels with the top label indicating the child's current Lexile reading level. The poor librarian was required to check the reading level on the cards against the books the children wanted to check out. If children picked a book that wasn't on their level, she had to take it and direct them to select another one. Imagine how it feels to hear you can't read a book you want to read. Imagine your entire class witnessing this exchange. How would you feel about reading? It's difficult to imagine how children can build self-efficacy or reading confidence under such systems.

## One Student's Story

Colby recently reconnected with a former student, now in high school, who told him about limitations being placed on his independent reading choices. To make matters worse, the young man admitted he wasn't reading much because of those limitations. So Colby recommended Jason Reynolds's compelling novel in verse, *A Long Way Down*. Colby had recently finished the book and believed it would be perfect to reconnect his former student with reading.

After recommending the book, Colby was dismayed to receive his student's response: "I can't read that book." Worried that this student might not have a fast way to access the book, Colby offered to send him a copy, but that wasn't the problem. "I cannot read the book because our reading program [at our school] doesn't have a test for it and it's not at my level." Imagine not being able to pass a book along to a child at the right time because it was so new that the school's computer-based reading management program didn't have a multiple-choice test for it!

As upsetting as this was, Colby still worked to find a book this student could read—searching the program's website for "acceptable" books, creating a list of recommendations, and sharing it. For some readers it takes only one book to help them fall in love, or fall back in love, with reading. When we limit reading choices based on the convenience of an online multiple-choice test, we are serving adults, not kids.

Again and again, we see reading level measures used to rank children, sort them into reading groups, identify "at-risk" readers, or generate grades. To what end? If we value a whole-child model of education, children's development of lifelong reading habits and skills should matter just as much as reading scores. Requiring students to read books "at their level" at all times derails intrinsic motivation to read, which is driven by interest, choice, and reader's purpose.

Chapter 5: On the Level: Some Truths About Text Leveling Systems          53

# Level Books, Not Students

While we don't want students laboring to read text that is too difficult for them to comprehend, or burning through books that offer little intellectual challenge, we must be mindful of how reading level systems affect children's reading identities. Reading levels are meant to guide, not limit or define children's reading choices. Consider what reading level systems offer and what they don't.

## Reading levels apply to the texts children read, not the children themselves.

Reading level instruments like Lexile were designed to measure text complexity. These tools were not created to assess children. Reading levels are tools meant to guide teachers' instruction and text selection, not labeling systems for kids.

Irene Fountas and Gay Su Pinnell, the co-creators of the F&P Text Level Gradient™, have expressed concerns about the misuse of the leveling framework. In a 2017 interview in *School Library Journal*, they emphasized, "It is our belief that levels have no place in classroom libraries, in school libraries, in public libraries, or on report cards." Fountas and Pinnell insist that children should not use reading levels as limits when selecting books to read (Parrott, 2017).

## The "right" level varies from reading event to reading event, and from reader to reader.

We cannot disregard each reader's preparedness when determining the accessibility of a text. Physical health, alertness, stress, engagement, and our self-concept about reading all affect our ability to read any given text (Schwanenflugel & Knapp, 2017). Reading is a transaction between the reader and the text, and we don't walk into new texts empty-handed. Readers bring their background knowledge, culture, gender, life experiences, and prior literacy experiences into every text, which affect their comprehension and motivation to read. The quality of the text drives our ability to read it, too. Well-written, engaging books are more accessible to read. Text formatting and book design features like font, page size, visuals, and color can influence text readability from reader to reader. Preferences and experiences vary. We don't all access the same text in the same way.

## Reading level systems are scaffolds, and scaffolds are temporary.

When you go to Barnes & Noble, you do not see adult readers looking for the blue dots or using the Five Finger Rule to find books to read. You don't ask the bookstore clerk to help you find books at your Lexile. The goal of all teaching is independence. How are we guiding children toward independent reading lives? Children should be able to select a book for their own purposes and determine if they can probably read it. Dependence on reading level as the primary criterion guiding book selection impedes reading independence long term.

Children need modeling and instruction in how to preview and select reading material like readers really do. (We share strategies for teaching and practicing book selection skills in Chapters 7, 8, and 9.) We cannot presume children know how to pick books for themselves. According to Scholastic's *2016 Kids and Family Reading Report*, the majority of children and adolescents ages 6 to 17 report that they struggle to find enjoyable books to read and that the adults in their lives underestimate how hard it is for them to find and select books (Scholastic, 2016).

## Conspicuous labeling of book levels in libraries violates students' academic privacy.

According to the American Library Association's Position Statement on the Labeling of Books with Reading Levels, students' reading levels are confidential academic information—like grades and test scores (2011). When students are required to select books from a visibly leveled collection, their information becomes public to everyone in sight—including other students, staff, and library volunteers. Labeling levels also alters children's book browsing behaviors and pushes reading level ahead of more authentic book selection criteria like author, genre, or topic. School and classroom libraries should be places where children can select books without restrictions or shame.

We are especially concerned about how reading leveling systems are used to evaluate and limit the reading lives of children who need additional reading support and intervention instruction. **For children reading significantly below grade level, reading level systems become limits on their reading lives and perpetual reminders that they aren't "good" readers.** Instead of considering what supports developing readers need to access the texts they want to read, we force children to read scripted texts and test prep—denying fragile, developing readers access to the engaging texts and literacy opportunities their on-grade-level peers enjoy. Literacy intervention specialist Mary Howard offers tangible methods for supporting at-risk readers—reinforcing that best practices benefit all readers.

CHANGE IN ACTION

**Mary Howard**

# Six Ways to Increase Reading Volume for the Children Who Need It Most

If interventions usurp the critical role of voluminous reading, we ignore what should be a central feature of interventions. If we redefine interventions in a way that emphasizes reading volume, we will also redefine "reading success." With this critical goal in mind, I suggest six "Intervention Heart Goals" that reclaim reading volume for the children who need it most:

## INTERVENTION HEART GOAL #1: AVOID DATA-ONLY EVALUATION

We often assign children to RTI support tiers based solely on numbers. Because assessment drives instruction, we want to ensure that we consider a range of information—both quantitative and qualitative. For example, if we assess speed only, then we increase the likelihood that children will participate in interventions designed to promote speed. By evaluating data using varied sources of formative assessment information, we could redesign our interventions from a more expansive, reader-centered perspective.

## INTERVENTION HEART GOAL #2: RECOMMIT TO THE FIRST LINE OF DEFENSE

When we opt for a pull-out approach, we run the risk of sacrificing valuable reading opportunities in Tier 1, or the general education setting. An RTI design obligates us to ensure that interventions beyond Tier 1 offer "in addition to" rather than "instead of" support. Such practices rob children of valuable time with the person who should know them best—their classroom teacher—in the classroom where they have the best chance to engage with books. Pull- out approaches ignore the reality that we cannot make up in 30 minutes what happens during the other six hours, particularly if our efforts from both sides are devoid of passion-driven reading.

### INTERVENTION HEART GOAL #3: DEDICATE BLOCKS OF "SACRED TIME"

RTI has created an intervention revolving door, limiting opportunities where all children can gather and read and discuss books together. We cannot create a learning community where volume, choice, and in-class instructional support is a priority if children are rarely in the same room at the same time. Schools need dedicated blocks of "sacred time" that is "intervention-free." This would optimize time for meaningful instruction and ensure real reading takes place.

### INTERVENTION HEART GOAL #4: EMBRACE DAILY LITERACY NON-NEGOTIABLES

Children who need greater volume in their reading often miss those opportunities, as engaged reading and choice are viewed as expendable in favor of interventions. Read-aloud is an intervention as we immerse students in "ear books" they may be unable to read on their own. Independent reading is an intervention that invites children into celebratory experiences beckoning them into rich reading lives. Peer collaboration is an intervention as meaningful dialogue affords time to think more deeply about reading in the company of others. These experiences maximize volume while inviting all children into our community of learners.

### INTERVENTION HEART GOAL #5: REDESIGN INTERVENTIONS TO LIFT READING VOLUME

Interventions within or beyond Tier 1 should raise the volume of reading using engaging texts rather than limiting volume. Indeed, reading volume should be the central feature of interventions, with about two-thirds of the lesson time focused on purposeful engaged reading, discussion, and faded support. Interventions should be synonymous with voluminous authentic reading using the most engaging texts available. As Stephanie Harvey and Annie Ward remind us, "The best intervention is a good book" (Harvey & Ward, 2017).

### INTERVENTION HEART GOAL #6: CELEBRATE INFORMAL PROFESSIONAL CONVERSATIONS

Successful interventions thrive on collegial conversations that put us all on the same "professional page" and inspire us to explore how we could increase volume across the learning day. Reading volume should be our priority for all children. Let's rethink Response to Intervention as "Responsive Thoughtful Instruction" with heart.

I'd say that's an RTI renewal worth exploring!

# Closing Thoughts

The primary drivers of voluminous independent reading are choice and interest over everything else. As reading mentors, we can suggest books based on children's interests that we think they can successfully read. If a child selects a book we suspect they cannot read independently, what strategies can we teach or what resources can we provide that will help them read it anyway? Do we know other books that might interest this reader, but are more accessible to read? Can we collaborate with a librarian to increase our book knowledge or help us match children with books? Our informed guidance supports young readers long term, and they must learn the skills and strategies required to self-select books without leveling systems—like readers really do.

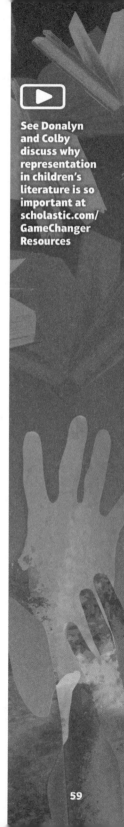

See Donalyn and Colby discuss why representation in children's literature is so important at scholastic.com/ GameChanger Resources

# Cultural and Social Access to Books: The Need for Representation in Children's Literature

*"I was raised in Harlem. I never found a book that took place in Harlem. I never had a church like mine in a book. I never had people like the people I knew. People who could not find their lives in books and celebrated felt bad about themselves. I needed to write to include the lives of these young people."*

**—WALTER DEAN MYERS**

In 1965, Dr. Nancy Larrick published the results of a three-year study, examining books published for children from 1962 to 1965. Looking at thousands of books, Larrick found that less than seven percent of them featured African American characters (Larrick, 1965). Discussions about the inadequate and often insensitive representation of historically marginalized groups in children's and young adult literature reach back to its origins.

Fast-forward more than 50 years, and things haven't changed much. People of color, indigenous people, people from global nationalities, cultures, and ethnicities (other than white Europeans and Americans), people with disabilities, people of various religions and spiritual beliefs (other than Christian or Jewish), and people on the spectrum of sexual orientations and gender identities remain underrepresented (or represented poorly) in books published for young readers. No matter how good our intentions may be, children often do not have access to books reflecting their experiences and their families. The absence of a voice is judgment against it. When children cannot see themselves or their families represented in the books we offer, we communicate that their stories don't matter, or worse, warrant shame. The lack of relevant, positive, affirming books for every child often perpetuates stereotypes, children's self-perceptions of "otherness," and institutional and social constructs that marginalize and oppress many people.

# Representation in Children's and Young Adult Literature

Dr. Rudine Sims Bishop coined the metaphor "mirrors, windows, and sliding glass doors" to explain the role books play in broadening young readers' understanding of other people and themselves:

> Books are sometimes windows, offering views of worlds that may be real or imagined, familiar or strange. These windows are also sliding glass doors, and readers have only to walk through in imagination to become part of whatever world has been created or recreated by the author. When lighting conditions are just right, however, a window can also be a mirror. Literature transforms human experience and reflects it back to us, and in that reflection we can see our own lives and experiences as part of the larger human experience. Reading, then, becomes a means of self-affirmation, and readers often seek their mirrors in books (Bishop, 1990).

In the past, some corners of the publishing industry claimed that diverse books appealed to a limited audience and didn't sell well enough to be profitable. This isn't true (Gilmore, 2015). More teachers, librarians, parents, and caregivers would buy and share diverse books with children if they had a wide range of high-quality books from which to choose—and if they were well informed about the availability of those books.

We educators need to do more to support families and children. We cannot continue reading about the same four notable African Americans every year during

Black History Month, checking a diversity box on our lesson plans, and moving on. Diversity isn't a trend or a box to check. It must be woven into and through everything we do. Many educators of color have been advocating for children and their rights to inclusive books for years; all of us must follow their lead, work together, and look for ways to include a wide range of voices and perspectives throughout our classroom instruction.

The authors of *No More Culturally Irrelevant Teaching*, all women of color, challenge us to consider students whose classrooms do not offer texts that reflect them: "Imagine that practically every day you go to school, you are asked to read or listen to something that is not representative of who you are, of your family, or of your community" (Souto-Manning, et al., 2018). Why would students engage in the classroom work? Why would they engage in reading? Teacher Stacey Riedmiller urges us to make access a priority: "If children cannot see themselves in the books they have access to within the walls of their classroom—this is harming children."

Every book we read aloud, share through lessons, discuss with students, promote in book talks, display in the classroom and library, and include on book lists offers an opportunity to enrich children's lives with the experiences of many people from all walks of life. Every child deserves to see themselves, their families, and their communities in books and learn about the lives of others. It is unlikely we are engaging many children in reading when they never see their realities portrayed positively and frequently in texts they encounter at school (Fleming, et al., 2016).

## We Need Diverse Books and Other Organizations of Change

Change is slow, but moving in the right direction. In 2014, a network of children's authors and illustrators launched the nonprofit organization, We Need Diverse Books (weneeddiversebooks.org), as a grassroots effort to address systemic inequities in the children's publishing industry and the inadequate or harmful representations of many groups in children's and young adult books. Working with publishers, editors, agents, booksellers, book lovers, educators, and librarians, We Need Diverse Books promotes the publications of diverse authors and illustrators and actively works to amplify their voices. The organization provides resources such as high-quality book review sources, book lists, book-talking kits, and articles through social media and its website. It also leads initiatives to recruit diverse artists and advocates through its grant, internship, and award programs. To explore additional diverse social media accounts and online platforms, please see scholastic.com/GameChangerResources.

Through the work of We Need Diverse Books, as well as other organizations such as Social Justice Books (socialjusticebooks.org), the number of diverse books published has increased. Many publishing companies have formed diversity teams and initiatives to solicit manuscripts from underrepresented authors and illustrators, diversify their editorial staff, and publish and promote quality diverse books.

However, there's still a long way to go. The Cooperative Children's Book Center of the School of Education at the University of Wisconsin-Madison has been documenting for over 30 years children's books by indigenous creators and creators of color and representations of various demographic groups. Although the publication of diverse voices and perspectives is increasing, the industry still favors predominantly male, white authors and illustrators. The majority of children's books published each year featuring diverse protagonists continue to be written by white, cisgender, able-bodied authors, which means publishing opportunities remain limited for historically marginalized creators and their lived experiences remain largely unrecognized (CCBC, 2018). You can learn more about CCBC's history, evaluation process, and data at its website (ccbc.education.wisc.edu/books/pcstats.asp), as well as recommended reading for educators and researchers and resources such as "50 Multicultural Books Every Child Should Know."

## Rethinking the Topics, Locations, and Audiences of Diverse Books

The topics of many diverse books being published for children also warrant concern. In too many books, the diverse qualities of the main characters, their families, or their communities are at the heart of the conflict or problem that must be overcome. Children and adolescents should not always encounter messaging that what makes them diverse is negative or a source of conflict.

Furthermore, too many books center diverse peoples and human rights concerns in the past—as if prejudice, bigotry, misogyny, and racism were issues resolved long ago, or that Native and enslaved peoples no longer exist in contemporary society. Yes, books about the civil rights movement, slavery, immigration, urban violence, the Holocaust, the Stonewall riots, the Trail of Tears, suffragettes, and Pearl Harbor should be written and shared with children, but these stories cannot be the only stories children see that feature underrepresented people. Children need everyday stories where diversity is not seen as a struggle or plot point, stories where diverse characters and subjects take center stage, stories where diversity is celebrated.

One of Donalyn's students, Hailey, read avidly but avoided historical fiction. Curious, Donalyn asked Hailey during a reading conference if they should work on finding books that would interest her. Hailey, who identifies as African American, told Donalyn, "I hate historical fiction, Mrs. Miller. All of the books with kids who look like me are depressing. I want books like Harry Potter, but none of those books have black kids. Can you help me find some?" Hailey wanted books about magic, not slavery. Unfortunately, there are a lot more books featuring enslaved children than black magicians.

Often, diverse books are relegated to separate sections of the library, placed on separate book lists, or used to support instruction during observances and celebrations like Chinese New Year or Hanukkah, but rarely integrated into the curriculum the rest of the year.

In many instances, teachers and librarians seek out diverse books if their students are predominantly children of color, but don't feel the impetus to do so if their students are white. Yes, children of color need to read books with people of color as main characters and featured subjects. White children need to read them, too. As Dr. Sims Bishop reminds us, "[Children from dominant social groups] need books that will help them understand the multicultural nature of the world they live in, and their place as a member of just one group, as well as their connections to all other humans."

We are not just teaching the people our students are right now. We are teaching the global citizens they will become. Reading diverse texts provides students with opportunities to "live through" and not just have "knowledge about" the lives of people with different experiences and perspectives than our own (Short & Fox, 2004).

Multicultural texts should not be used to support lesson plans that reduce complex cultures to stereotypes, or to meet some didactic moral and historical purposes for education, while ignoring the value of different perspectives and voices the rest of the time. All children need to read about a wide range of lives and experiences—both similar to and different than their own. The books we publish, buy, share, and promote shape the narratives that children write about themselves and the world.

## Doing What We Can Do

As two white educators, we don't claim to be experts on diversity, social justice, or culturally responsive teaching. However, we are committed to growing our practices and perspectives by seeking out, reading, and sharing diverse writers and their stories; expanding our networks of professional colleagues and influencers to include a variety of voices and roles; listening to educators from many communities with a variety of perspectives and experiences; recognizing and overcoming our own biases; and improving our understanding and empathy.

Increasing children's access to books and other media that celebrate and amplify the mosaic of people who inhabit our world is going to require white teachers like us to care more and work harder. As fifth-grade teacher Jessica Lifshitz reminds us, "We white teachers, of mostly white students, we have a lot of work to do." We know that increasing access to diverse books won't single-handedly dismantle an entire educational system built on racism, prejudice, and inequity, but adding more diverse books to collections and classroom instruction will bring schools one step closer to more meaningful, culturally responsive teaching.

# Creating More Classroom Access to Diverse Literature

As we commit to long-term work, here are some ideas for getting started:

**Read a lot of diverse texts written for children and young adults.**
Seek out review sources and book lists created by educators, librarians, and scholars from underrepresented groups. On the following pages, you'll find Kimberly Parker talking about books that celebrate the experiences of black boys and Anna Osborn reviewing books featuring Filipino characters. You can find additional recommendations at scholastic.com/GameChangerResources. Book lists like these contain trustworthy recommendations because their creators not only study children's and young adult literature and how to engage young readers, but also evaluate every book through the lens of their lived experiences, checking for accuracy, positive representations, and relevance.

**CHANGE IN ACTION**

Kimberly N. Parker

# Books Celebrating Black Boy Joy and Other Important Feelings

Children's and young adult literature featuring boys of African descent does exist and is quite robust (though we can *always* use more). The following list provides a range of texts to help you help boys to see themselves in literature; to help them join important conversations about gender and masculinity; and to help you build your classroom libraries with inclusive texts that benefit the literacy lives of *all* students. Note: Most authors and illustrators are of African descent to reflect the importance of #ownvoices, an online movement to increase the publication of stories about marginalized people, written by marginalized people, that accurately and sensitively reflect the racial backgrounds of children depicted in the texts.

## PRIMARY

*Crown: An Ode to the Fresh Cut*, Derrick Barnes and Gordon James (illustrator)

*Willie's Not the Hugging Kind*, Joyce Durham Barrett and Pat Cummings (illustrator)

*Before There Was Mozart: The Story of Joseph Boulogne, Chevalier de Saint-George*, Lesa Cline-Ransome and James Ransome (illustrator)

*Max and the Tag-Along Moon*, Floyd Cooper

*I'm a Big Brother Now*, Katura Hudson and Sylvia Walker (illustrator)

*Large Fears*, Myles Johnson and Kendrick Daye (illustrator)

*Kevin and His Dad; Jonathan and His Mommy*, Irene Smalls and Michael Hays (illustrator)

## INTERMEDIATE

*What Color Is My World? The Lost History of African American Inventors*, Kareem Abdul-Jabbar

*Booked*, Kwame Alexander

*Tears of a Tiger*, Sharon Draper

*Clayton Byrd Goes Underground*, Rita Williams-Garcia

*Thirteen Ways of Looking at a Black Boy*, Tony Medina and 13 artists

*The Stars Beneath Our Feet*, David Barclay Moore

*Ghost*, Jason Reynolds

*This Kid Can Fly: It's About Ability (Not Disability)*, Aaron Philip and Tonya Bolden

### YOUNG ADULT

*Tyrell*, Coe Booth

*The Pact: Three Young Men Make a Promise and Fulfill a Dream*, Sampson Davis, George Jenkins, and Rameck Hunt

*Strange Fruit: Uncelebrated Narratives From Black History*, Joel Christian Gill

*The First Part Last*, Angela Johnson

*Riding Chance*, Christine Kendall

*Boy21*, Matthew Quick

*Long Way Down*, Jason Reynolds

*Don't Call Us Dead*, Danez Smith

*X: A Novel*, Ilyasah Shabazz and Kekla Magoon

---

**CHANGE IN ACTION**

**Anna Osborn**

## Books With Filipino Characters

Being one of almost four million Filipinos in the United States is a source of pride for me, but growing up, it was nearly impossible to find children's and young adult books with Filipino characters or stories about the Philippines. When I talk with my students about books as mirrors and windows, I share my childhood experience with them and the excitement I felt when, as an adult, I began collecting books featuring Filipino characters. The books are every bit a window for my students as they are for me. See my list of books we enjoy discussing at scholastic.com/GameChangerResources.

**Follow thought leaders in the fields of social and restorative justice, culturally responsive teaching, and diversity in education and publishing.**
We have included a short list of websites and professional books as a launching point (see scholastic.com/GameChangerResources). The authors of those websites and books will lead you to many more resources and topics of study. We suggest following social media hashtags, too, such as #weneeddiversebooks, #wndb, #ownvoices, and #disrupttexts.

**Evaluate your classroom and school libraries for diverse representation.**
Whose voices and stories are underrepresented or missing? Are representations in the books accurate or do they perpetuate misconceptions and stereotypes? Lee and Low, a small press that publishes diverse books, has created an eight-part protocol for teachers and librarians to use when evaluating collections. Find it here: blog.lee andlow.com/2014/05/22/checklist-8-steps-to-creating-a-diverse-book-collection/.

Teacher Lynsey Burkins regularly evaluates her classroom library for diverse representations and books reflecting her students' identities, and building an inclusive classroom community.

### *CHANGE IN ACTION*

**Lynsey Burkins**

## Classroom Library Audit

Helping students discover who they are as readers and build their reading identities is a treasured goal of mine. I strive to help students see themselves as people who can read to see themselves and others and who can read for enjoyment and empowerment. This requires a diverse classroom library.

Recently I had a student ask me, "Mrs. Burkins, Jackie is reading *Sofia Martinez*—she really likes it. Where are the books with Indian girls?" Sadly, I had only one to offer her.

I always tell my students they should seek to find books in which they can see themselves. It is my responsibility to surround them with books allowing for this to happen. My student's comment was a gut check for me. I realized I had to create a system for evaluating our classroom library.

As we support students to become good citizens, we must expand our definition of reading identity to include opportunities for them to interact with texts and their world at the same time. The Social Identity Wheel Exercise below was created to help individuals identify and reflect on the identities they hold and how those identities intersect and shape the way they interact in our world.

As a teacher, this was a powerful exercise because it helped me reflect on my influence as an educator based on the identities I acknowledge most and least. It became evident that my identities I acknowledged least were causing me to miss students and inadvertently silence them. I didn't want that to happen, of course—so I went to work to overcome it.

I adapted the idea of The Social Identity Wheel Exercise to help me think about books in my classroom library.

Around the wheel are social identities we all hold. As I learn more about my students, I highlight the identities that they hold, and I think about books I have

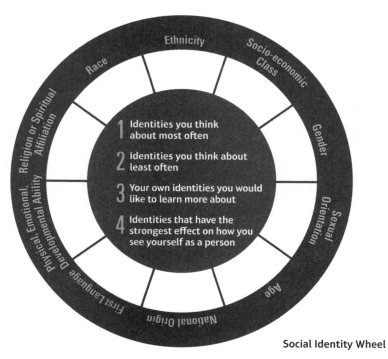

**Social Identity Wheel**

Adapted from "Voices of Discovery" by Intergroup Relations Center, Arizona State University

*Game Changer! Book Access for All Kids*

that might be a mirror. I look for issue-based books because they are important and they are a great way to build empathy, but reading them should not be the only way children see themselves or others. So I also look for incidental books, in which students can see themselves in incidental ways, and their specific identity is mentioned without necessarily being the "issue."

I begin the audit by taking a look at the library, and asking myself these reflective questions:

- What identities are most prevalent in our books?
- What identities are least evident and even missing?
- Do the percentage of books around an identity match the percentage of students in my class who hold that identity?
- What do the books in my classroom library say about the readers in the room?

These questions help me identify the "blind spots" in our classroom library. Sometimes I add or change identities on the wheel because the wheel is fluid. As I create the space and time to listen to my students, and notice needs that arise from them, I modify the wheel based on their input.

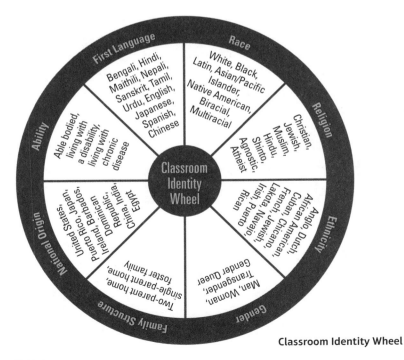

**Classroom Identity Wheel**

(Courtesy of Lynsey Burkins)

> As educators we are charged with maintaining a classroom library that impacts the many faces in front of us. We must be accountable to ourselves, to our profession, and most importantly to our students, and surround them with books that allow them to stand taller than they did when they first walked through our door.

**Reconsider texts used for classroom instruction.** How often do our students encounter contemporary voices, popular culture, and current events in the texts they read and discuss? Do the classic or traditional texts we share include stereotypes, historical inaccuracies or revisions, or missing perspectives? Stacey Riedmiller believes we should challenge ourselves to update the books we have used for years. "If the books in your classroom library only reflect stories you value, they may be harming children. When we say, 'I always start the year with this read-aloud,' or 'This title is the best to teach character change,' we are limiting students because we're exposing them only to what's familiar to us. Each year, we are blessed with a brand new group of students. These children bring their interests, culture, life experiences, and background knowledge into the mix. It is our job to honor these individuals by letting them know that we see them."

Teachers and literacy leaders Pernille Ripp and Jessica Lifshitz tap into their experiences with their own children to inform their understanding of diverse books and the importance of children and adolescents having mirrors, windows, and sliding glass doors—both at home and school.

**CHANGE IN ACTION**

**Pernille Ripp**

# Let's Not Default to White

My children are surrounded by books. In every room, everywhere, books are a vital thread weaving us together as a family. From the moment they could carry anything, my children carried books, waddling behind my husband and me, begging for us to read just one more page, for just one more shared moment of story. Of imagination. Of discovery about the world and everyone in it. And we obliged, plopping down on the floor, the couch, wherever, as we opened books they brought us.

My children are descendants of Danish Vikings: blue-eyed, blonde-haired, tall children who sound like Americans, but blend naturally into the landscape of my home nation of Denmark whenever we visit. Whenever we crack open new books, images of kids who look just like them greet us. White kids peer out from the pages as they battle their brothers, build tree forts, or miss their teddy bears. White kids and their everyday stories are what my kids see almost every day, and what all kids who read see every day.

White children represent everyday life experiences: eating dinner, spending time with friends, going on adventures. The stories that are supposed to represent the world predominantly feature white, cisgender, able-minded and -bodied, heteronormative families. Several years ago it struck me, as my children and I cuddled up to read a picture book featuring Christmas shenanigans, that once again there was no reason the characters in the book should be white— and yet they were, because no one had thought to do otherwise. We default to white.

So it's on us—parents and families. We must demand more diverse representation in our children's books: representation of differently structured families, of different skin colors, different religions, of diverse heritage, of disability, of nonbinary genders. My own children's skin color is not typical in their classrooms, so why should it be in the books they read?

We, as parents, must start with the books we share. We must become critical evaluators of the canon we establish in our homes. We must not just share our favorites without question, but look through the lens of what they present to our children. We need to invite conversation with our children about what they see and what they don't see. Ask them if this is representative of the world they live in, and if not, ask them how they would fix it.

So go through your children's bookshelves and see who is represented and how, and who is not. Support authors who write from underrepresented experiences. We must do this work in our classrooms as well, but it starts within our homes—by reading books, our children begin to learn who they are. If we want children to grow up believing in, and fighting for, equality for all, then it starts with the stories we read together.

Jessica Lifshitz

## Access to Books Is Access to the Lives of Others

Educators know children need access to books offering mirrors, windows, and sliding glass doors (Bishop, 1990). But for those of us who live in marginalized communities, our desire to see ourselves in books is almost matched by our desire for others to see us in books, too. We want to be understood and we know that books help foster empathy.

My own daughter needed this understanding from others when she was just three years old. We had taken her to the park and she'd run off to play with a little boy. I could hear their conversation. The little boy pointed to a man and said, "That's my daddy!"

My daughter then pointed to my wife and me and said, "Oh, that's my mommy and mama!"

"Well, where's your daddy?" he asked with no unkindness in his voice, but in a way that made my daughter stop and become quiet.

"I don't have one. I have a mommy and a mama." The little boy looked over at us and then back at her. And as I watched him take in this family that he did not understand, I tried to resist the urge to run over and swoop up my daughter and protect her from this moment.

But I needn't have worried. The little boy paused and said, "Okay. You want to go on the slide now?" And off they went. The moment had passed. But I knew others would come, and not all would be so innocent.

What if the child asking her to explain herself had first encountered a family that looks like ours in a book? What if that child had the opportunity to ask questions of a teacher or another grown-up before looking to my three-year-old to explain our family?

We know more because of the books we read and the stories we hear. As educators, we have the power to change what our students know and understand about the world through the books that we share with them. We can bring books to our students that push them beyond the limits of their experiences and into the world.

In my classroom, I have worked hard to create a library that not only reflects my students' lives but that reflects the wide perspectives of others. Not only have I worked to bring more books into our classroom, but I have also worked to make sure that those books are accurately and positively reflecting the people with whom my students share this world. And I have gotten rid of books that present negative or problematic representations of people or groups of people. When my students encounter people in the world that remind them of characters in the books they have read, they are welcoming because the images they carry are positive, accurate, and complex, and push against commonly held stereotypes.

Once the right books are in our classrooms, we must ensure our students engage with them. When I choose books to share with my students, I make sure to talk about books such as *Star-Crossed* by Barbara Dee, *The Other Boy* by M. G. Hennessey, *Refugee* by Alan Gratz, *Amal Unbound* by Aisha Saeed, *Ghost Boys* by Jewell Parker Rhodes, and *Ghost* by Jason Reynolds. Every time I talk about one of those books, I am talking about more than a book. I'm talking about a life that my students may be unfamiliar with.

When I choose a mentor text for a writing lesson, I think about the writing strategies I can introduce to my students, but I also think about the human beings I can introduce to them. If I want my students to learn to write powerful descriptions of setting, I might choose to read aloud *Last Stop on Market Street* by Matt de la Peña. If I want to them to learn to use descriptive language, I might choose to read *Yo Soy Muslim* by Mark Gonzales.

As we use these books to teach our students, we need to show them how to be open to experiences that differ from their own, how to listen without judgment when someone shares their truth, how to ask questions and seek answers instead of allowing assumptions to fill in what they do not know, and how to seek out a variety of stories from a variety of perspectives so that they do not develop stereotypes.

The world is filled with incredible humans whose stories have been kept out of our classrooms for far too long. And it has caused too many people harm. It is up to us to reverse the damage, which means giving our students access to books that give them access to the lives of those who have not always been welcome.

Please know that there are those of us who hope, with everything in our hearts, that people like us are welcomed into classrooms and homes so that the next child my daughter meets at the playground understands her family because that child has met one like hers within the pages of a book.

# Closing Thoughts

All children deserve to see their experiences and their families reflected in the books they read. All children need to learn about the lives of other people through their books, too. Reading, sharing, and discussing texts from many voices and perspectives fosters empathy and awareness, and helps young people become participatory, inclusive citizens who care about the world and other people.

See Donalyn and Colby discuss the importance of knowing children's literature at scholastic.com/ GameChanger Resources

# Knowing Children's and Young Adult Literature: The Key to Matching Readers With Books

*"I like to know that my teachers love reading because that lets students know they really care about it, and they want me to read, too."*

**—BREH, FOURTH GRADER**

Donalyn owns more books than she can read. Several bookcases in her house store books she plans to read "someday." Book stacks wedge into every discrete corner of her house. No matter how many books she reads or gives away, these piles don't shrink. Colby is constantly adjusting his to-read stack. Each time he finishes a book, he agonizes over which one he will read next. Selecting one book means the others have to wait. Author Maud Casey said, "I was born with a reading list I will never finish," and we can relate. Keeping up with all of the books we want to read for our learning and enjoyment (or share with other readers) becomes daunting and unmanageable at times. Although we read hundreds of books each year, our students still outread us and often ask about books we haven't seen or read.

As educators mentoring young readers, building our knowledge of books available for children and adolescents to read remains an ongoing part of our professional development. We occasionally meet educators and caregivers who deride children's and young adult literature—claiming it lacks the literary merit or rigor of texts published for adults. It doesn't take long to determine that these naysayers haven't read many books published for young people and have no basis to criticize their value or importance. We have learned a lot about literature, the human experience, and the world through books written for young people. Don't knock it until you've tried it. Teachers who read children's and young adult literature are more capable of recommending books to students and building stronger reading communities (Clark & Teravainen, 2015). Reading many of the books our students read gives us launching points for discussions about books, reading, and the topics and issues that concern them.

Our students and their families trust our suggestions, and we don't take this influence lightly. Parents and caregivers often lack information and resources to help their children find books. When we can pair both our relationships with families and our experiences with books for their children to read, we can support our students' reading lives long after they leave our classrooms. Offering this personal support requires us to read widely, investigate credible book recommendations and review sources, and connect with scholars in the field and other readers.

# Building Your Book-Knowledge Muscle

Many educators, librarians, and caregivers ask us how to increase their knowledge of children's books and remain current about books for their students and children to read. We have learned a lot since our teaching careers began. Here are some tips for building up your book knowledge. Pick one or two suggestions to start, and add more as it suits your needs.

## Dedicate Daily Time for Reading

If you want to increase your book knowledge, you must commit to reading more. While reading reviews and researching books can improve and extend your book knowledge, there is no substitute for reading the books yourself and determining how to share them with other readers. (Check out Kristin Ziemke's tips in Chapter 8 for fitting more reading time into your life.)

## Read Strategically

**Accept your inability to read everything you want.** There are thousands of books published for young readers every year. You cannot possibly read every book that looks interesting to you. You are going to miss some great books. You are going to read some amazing books, too. Enjoy your reading life and set aside your FOMO (fear of missing out)!

**Abandon books that are not working for you.** Don't waste your limited reading time and mental energy reading books you don't appreciate. What do you need from a book? How long will you read a book before deciding not to finish? What do you notice about the books you abandon? What do you notice about the books you finish? Set personal guidelines, and feel free to ditch a book if it doesn't meet your needs. This reflection improves our interactions with young readers when we discuss book abandonment with them (Miller, 2013).

**Abandon series, too, if necessary.** You are not required to finish a series just because you start one. You do not have to read every book in the Warriors series in order to recommend them to students. If you're enjoying reading an entire series, go right ahead. Binge reading a series has its own pleasures, but don't feel you have to slog through every book if you're no longer invested.

**Alternate book lengths.** Intimidated by the 500-page epic fantasy tome on your shelf? Pick a shorter book. Your reading stamina flags? Pick a shorter book. You haven't finished a book in a month? Pick a shorter book. Making brisk pace through a book fills you with accomplishment and keeps your reading momentum going when you cannot make a long-term commitment to a lengthy book.

## Read Winners and Nominees on National and State Award Lists

The American Library Association's Youth Media Awards, the National Book Awards, and many educational organizations like the National Council of Teachers of English (NCTE) and the National Science Teachers Association (NSTA) select outstanding books and media for young people. Many state library associations create recommended reading lists of children's and young adult literature each year, too. While any award list must be critically evaluated for representation, bias, perspective, and agenda, such lists can keep your book knowledge current and heighten awareness of the authors and illustrators creating exemplary books for young readers.

## Read Widely

Select titles from a range of perspectives, voices, formats, topics, and genres. You never know what book will spark a child's interests or needs or find its way into your classroom instruction. Challenge yourself to read outside of your preferred genres and authors. Adults cannot allow our reading preferences to limit children's access to books or communicate that we value certain readers and certain types of reading more than others. The more widely we read, the more likely we can lead children to relevant, engaging books.

## Befriend a Librarian

Librarians know about the latest books and resources and can support educators and caregivers in locating texts that support both curricular and independent reading goals. School and public librarians can also connect you with books in various formats like audiobooks and ebooks and help you locate credible book review resources.

## Ask Kids What You Should Read

If we see several kids reading a book that we have not read, we will track down a copy and read it. No matter how strong our book knowledge, the best people to recommend books to young readers are their peers.

## Browse Bookstores and Library Shelves

Independent booksellers and public librarians know the needs and reading preferences of their communities and possess extensive knowledge about books, resources, and book-related events. Casual browsing in bookstores and libraries has become a lost art. Colby doesn't have a bookstore in his county, and Donalyn's closest independent bookstore is 20 miles away. Many of our students have never been in a bookstore, and adults forgo trips to the library in favor of downloading books from library databases. Wandering bookshelves, paging through books, examining displays and recommendations, and chatting with other readers enhances the reading experience and reinforces the social nature of reading for many people. We have discovered so many books and creators we didn't know before while browsing shelves and talking with library and store staff.

## Read With Your Ears

Do you listen to music or podcasts while exercising or working? Do you have a long commute or spend time traveling? Downloading a few audiobooks to your phone or device provides boredom insurance and opportunities to squeeze in a few more books. Many students benefit from audiobooks, too. (Don't miss Dr. Antero Garcia's essay about audiobooks in Chapter 9.) Ask your public library about their audiobook database access. Search Audible, Amazon's audiobook service, by narrator when you find an enjoyable performer, and explore noteworthy productions from audiobook award lists like ALA's Odyssey Award and the Audio Publishers Association's Audie Award.

## Start a Book Club

Find a few colleagues or parents who share your interest in children's literature, and schedule regular meetings online or in person to discuss the books you read and ways to share them with young readers.

## Follow Reviewers' and Authors' Blogs

There are hundreds of book reviewers online who review children's and young adult books. Which books earn good reviews or appear in social media conversations? Which books seem like a good fit for your students? Which books fill a need in your community? While you can't read every blog and book review site, find a few that offer credible, comprehensive, easy-to-access information. In addition to Nerdy Book

Club (www.nerdybookclub.com), the blog we started in 2011, check out the list of recommendation and review sources collected from Donalyn and Colby's Facebook poll (shout out to everyone who provided recommendations!). To see our blog recommendations, go to scholastic.com/GameChangerResources.

## Attend Professional Development Workshops and Sessions on Literature for Young People

When attending conferences or workshops, we always look for children's and young adult literature sessions that introduce us to titles we might have missed, provide context and background information about creators and their work, or show us interesting ways to use books with students.

## Read Publications That Contain Book Reviews

With limited money to purchase books and limited time to read, you have to manage your resources. Reading review publications like *Horn Book*, *School Library Journal*, *Booklist*, and others provides high-quality background information on thousands of books. You can fine-tune your to-read piles and research books you haven't read yet.

Check your public library network or ask your school librarian about review resources.

Of course, our book knowledge matters only as much as it serves kids. How can we share books and resources with our students in ways that encourage them to read, improve their ability to choose books for themselves, and celebrate their reading experiences? Award-winning elementary principal and author Brad Gustafson shares tangible activities his staff implemented that illustrate how educators can leverage their book knowledge to launch school-wide conversations about books and increase students' reading engagement.

**CHANGE IN ACTION**

**Brad Gustafson**

# Learning Heartbeat

*When teachers share their love of reading, they influence students' reading lives and transform the heartbeat of their school.*

Our school's learning heartbeat has grown because of authentic reading practices promoted by passionate teacher leaders at our school. Here are nine ideas to spur your thinking and nurture your school's culture of literacy:

## 1. START A STUDENT-LED LITERACY PODCAST

This year we transformed office communications by converting the Principal's Podcast series into a "BookCast" video series. The videos feature students talking about the books they're reading over lunch. It is informal, authentic, and always full of laughs.

## 2. BUILD A BRIDGE BETWEEN STUDENT PASSIONS AND BOOKS

Students' LEGO book cover

Many of our students love making things at home. Whether they're playing LEGO, Minecraft, or helping to cook, they learn through making. We tap into this natural passion by creating a "Build-a-Book" LEGO wall. Students take turns reconstructing book covers together. This has become so popular that a local Eagle Scout is building us several more Build-a-Book centers for our hallways.

### 3. MODEL WHAT A VIBRANT READING LIFE LOOKS LIKE

You've probably heard the saying, "Readers are leaders." I incorporated this saying into my bulletin boards at least once a year, but I wasn't living it out myself. Other than our classroom read-alouds, I wasn't keeping current on new releases. With teachers around me always talking about the books they loved, I started reading more outside of school. Now, I can't stop recommending special books to specific students and staff.

### 4. EMBRACE THE POWER OF THE BOOK TALK

If there's one practice that I've seen spread book love more than any other, it's people talking about the books they love. When I share my monthly read-aloud selection, I often share a short book-talk video with our team in advance. This helps model what book talking might look like for students. My friend Jennifer LaGarde and I also started a national book-talk podcast called "30 Second Booktalk." It features a championship bracket with educators from around the world, but the best part is seeing so many students join us in sharing their book-talk videos via #30SecondBooktalk. You can follow the hashtag to learn more.

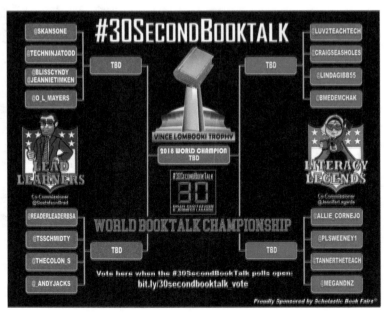

#30SecondBooktalk bracket

### 5. SHARE WHAT YOU'RE READING AND INVITE OTHERS TO DO THE SAME

Our team displays signs outside their classroom doors with the books we're reading. This practice spread to students, and now hundreds of students regularly update their personal book lists in spaces over their coat hooks. I love talking with kids as they're adding new titles!

(top) Dr. G is currently reading...

(left) Students' current reads

### 6. APPLY INNOVATION TO BEST PRACTICE

Several years ago, I ditched my traditional business cards and created something a little more student-centered. They're baseball-style cards featuring personal statistics like my current favorite book (*Forget Me Not*) and my favorite school lunch (mini-corn dogs). This year, I added augmented reality technology, so families can scan the picture on my card and watch a book-talk video.

Brad's business card

### 7. MAKE THE LOUNGE A LITERACY SANCTUARY

Teachers work ridiculously hard. They shouldn't have to work hard to find inspiring professional titles. We started a "Lounge Library" where teachers are free to take a book, leave a book, or request a new release or bestseller.

### 8. MAKE THE HEARTBEAT VISUAL

If the soul of your school could speak, what would it say? We took some of our school's core values and displayed them on the wall in our staff lounge with tiles. Of course, reading is well represented on the wall.

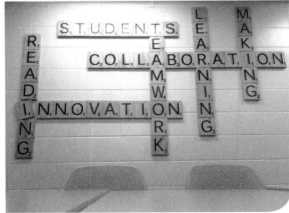

**(top)** Professional library for staff

**(bottom)** Core values wall

### 9. USE SOCIAL MEDIA AS LEARNING MEDIA

Our staff uses a hashtag to help our community of readers connect: #GWreads. This hashtag helps us collaborate on literacy-related ideas when we're not gathered together face-to-face, such as during school breaks.

Middle school principal LaQuita Outlaw has developed a daily ritual that shows her students and staff she is a reader and book promoter. She carries books wherever she goes!

**CHANGE IN ACTION**

LaQuita Outlaw

# One Way to Get Children (and Staff) Talking About Books

Talking about books is not hard when you love talking about books. But how do you get the reticent reader to jump on the reading train and stay on for the ride? One way is to hold a book in your hand as you walk around your school. Think about this—whenever someone is holding something, it's natural to be curious about what's in that person's hand. You secretly take a peek and quickly turn your head so your curiosity is not discovered. I've seen it happen over and over again as I walk around the building with my latest read nestled under my arm, or prominently displayed as I stand at my morning duty.

The first step is easy; grab a popular book that many students may have read. (I started with *Wonder* by R. J. Palacio.)

Then, proceed as usual—greet students in the hallway, travel from one destination to another, or walk around the cafeteria.

I am thrilled with the connections I've made with students revolving around books. Not only can I chat with students who have read the same book I am carrying, I often wind up book talking the book with students who haven't read it yet. From book recommendations to character critiques, I have created opportunities (that I might not have had otherwise) to freely engage in non-disciplinary conversations with our middle schoolers. The best part is that it happens so naturally. I am no longer "The Principal" when we talk; I am a book lover just like them. We talk for a minute, or we talk for the class period. We analyze characters, and we consider how the author developed the character from the start of the book until the end. We discuss what we expect to occur next. In the end, we've built a relationship and improved students' ability to critically examine text.

Although I am thankful for the interactions I have with the students, it's the conversations around books with the other staff members that I truly champion. You see, the more conversations that I have with the educators in the building, the more that conversations are likely to happen with children through these same educators, the teachers with whom they interact for at least 40 minutes every day. When teachers see a book in my hand, they often ask, "What are you reading now?" I am modeling for teachers the conversations they can have with students. It's a wonderful opportunity that does not go unnoticed. Holding *Fish in a Tree* by Lynda Mullaly Hunt, I share the struggles that Ally had and the teacher who helped her see that her current situation did not define her.

Or when I carry *Out of My Mind* by Sharon Draper, where the main character is disabled and learns to overcome her fears, I share a brief summary of the book and why I think they would enjoy reading it. I suggest they ask their students who has read the book. This simple action will demonstrate to students two things: *My teacher's a reader* and *we can talk about books*.

These conversations lead to discussions about other books teachers might personally connect with and can recommend to students, and I often see teachers holding books as they stand at their doors, too. You can hear students talking with teachers (and each other) about the books they're reading or have read in the past. Something so simple, reading books and sharing them, visibly becomes infectious—and we're not seeking a cure!

# Closing Thoughts

These two campus principals, LaQuita and Brad, exemplify how adults who work with young people and other educators can leverage their book knowledge to model what a reading life looks like, connect with students and colleagues, and strengthen their schools' reading communities. Children read more when they see adults in their lives reading.

# Dedicating Time for Reading at Home and School

See Donalyn and Colby discuss why it's so important to find enough time to read at home and at school at scholastic.com/ GameChanger Resources

*"Books make people quiet, yet they are so loud."*

**—NNEDI OKORAFOR**

In addition to book access, young readers benefit from daily reading time, opportunities to choose their own books, and relationships with reading peers and mentors. These conditions support reading engagement and growth both at school and home.

We make time for what we value. If we want our students and children to value reading, we must make it a priority. If we want them to own their reading lives, we have to encourage and support their interests and reading choices. If we want them to remain readers forever, we must model how to sustain a reading life in spite of all obstacles.

## Time to Read

Like any other skill, reading development requires practice. Children need lots of positive, engaging reading experiences to become readers. The more children read, the more their reading skills develop and their motivation and interest in reading increases, while children who do not read much do not develop strong reading skills and internal motivation to read. Time spent reading helps young readers fall into books and build fluency. When children read, they practice the reading skills they have learned while reading authentic texts. Children need time to read at school and home, and we must dedicate time in our schedules for it. **To develop reading confidence and competence, children must read widely and in volume.** This takes time. Lots of it.

## Dedicating Time for Independent Reading at School

The volume of independent, silent reading that students do in school is significantly related to gains in reading achievement (Swan, Coddington, Guthrie, 2010; Hiebert & Reutzel, 2010; Cunningham & Stanovich, 2003). Children who read 20 to 30 minutes a day score in the top rankings on standardized reading tests (Adams, 2006). Experts like Richard Allington recommend that elementary children spend two and a half hours a week—30 minutes a day—engaged in silent sustained reading (Allington, 2014). For teenagers, in classrooms with as little as 45 minutes for English class, teachers cannot provide 20 minutes of reading time on a daily basis. In those cases, carve out a minimum of 10 to 15 minutes every day rather than bursts of reading time once in a while.

During this reading time, children should be interacting with their teachers and classmates about what they are reading. Why do we need to set aside time for independent reading in class? Isn't this a waste of instructional time that would be better spent on whole-class instruction? Children benefit from whole-class and small-

group instruction, but independent reading time provides regular intervals for one-on-one instruction tailored to individual students' reading abilities and goals. Whole-class instruction is an efficient way to deliver content, but it's not an effective method for meeting the needs of individual children. Meeting with every reader in class provides targeted opportunities for both assessment and instruction that moves each child forward. Pairing both their knowledge of books and their knowledge of the children in their classrooms, English and language arts teachers are best suited to assess children's reading progress, negotiate reading goals, and provide individualized instruction.

Spending time reading alongside other readers reinforces reading as a community value worth investing time in. Setting aside daily reading time gives teachers opportunities to mentor students, assess what they know and what they need next, and facilitate reading relationships between children and their classmates. Regular reading conferences and classroom observations provide teachers with critical information about children's reading skill and their orientations toward reading. Through these interactions, we gain insight into children's reading habits, motivations, preferences, and needs.

**You have to be relentless and unwavering in your efforts to get kids to read. You can't let up on it.** When students are reading in class with you every day, it's hard to fake or skip reading forever. More than one student has admitted to Donalyn that she wore them down like water on a stone. "It's hard to come up with enough ways to fake read," Amber, a sixth grader, admitted to her. "You might as well just read. Besides, you have some pretty good stuff in here (to read)."

## Reading Observation Guide

You learn about your students—both as learners and as people—when you walk around the room observing and conferring with them during daily independent reading time. You can see:

- Who settles into reading time quickly and who takes longer.
- Who is reading a different book today than yesterday.
- Which books and series seem popular.
- Who is reading something surprising or unusual.
- Who initiates book conversations with classmates.
- Who is browsing the classroom library or needs to visit the school library.
- Who is writing about their reading.

What do students' reading habits and interests reveal to you? What do you see students doing or reading that piques your curiosity about them? What are some unobtrusive and focused ways to model, teach, and support students during reading time? Each observation gives teachers a springboard to launch a conversation with a student about their reading lives.

Beyond its academic benefits, dedicating time for reading in class gives teachers opportunities to build relationships with students. The books we read and discuss often become launching points for deeper conversations about students' past experiences, their lives at home, and their hopes for the future. A respite from the flood of noise from their families, teachers, and friends all day long, reading time provides young people with an opportunity to calm down, center themselves, rest, and be in their own heads for a bit. They can focus inward instead of responding to the needs and thoughts of the people around them.

Literacy coach and teacher Sara Ahmed describes how daily reading time helped her build a relationship of trust with a student who struggled to build positive relationships with adults at school. Reading time is about so much more than time.

**CHANGE IN ACTION**

**Sara K. Ahmed**

# One Minute. One Book. One Safe Space.

Elijah entered class the same way every day:
- Cut himself to the front of the line.
- Flipped his shoes off as fast as he could.
- Ignored all rules about walking safely and respectfully by sprinting, then catapulting himself onto the oversized bean-bag chair with his book in hand: *After Tupac and D Foster* by Jacqueline Woodson, given to him by his favorite teacher, our librarian Ms. Clayton (his second time reading it).

I gave up trying to correct his entry into our classroom once I realized that he was moving as fast as he could to get into a place he felt safe: lying down with a book that spoke to him. A place where he could be quiet with his thoughts, without adults (like me) trying to police his "loud," "angry," or "hyper" actions and thoughts. That was the language that preceded him before we even had the chance to see him—before he even had a chance to show us.

We began each 50-minute history class with what I call a soft start. Kids showed up either on time, a little late, or at Elijah's speed, and would reach for local newspapers, magazines such as *Sports Illustrated for Kids, Time for Kids, New York Times UpFront,* or the books in our library to enjoy at their own leisure for the first 10 minutes of class. Some would arrive with a text of their own already in hand; others would roam a bit, then settle. One of my favorite things to do was to have something ready for the roamers and the having-a-bad-weekers with a sticky note saying:

Hey! Thought of you.
<3 Ms. A.

I didn't always have time to do this, but sometimes I'd come across a text the night before or that morning that made me think of a particular student who I just knew would love it or hate it or connect to it the way that I did.

The kids always groaned when I tried to transition them to the lesson of the day. Nothing was better than that time they had to just be themselves—to pore over a magazine with a friend over her shoulder; to pass on the next book in a series; to check the box scores and highlights of the sports section; to size each other up, argue, then set up a game for later at recess so they could emulate the images they saw of KD or Carmelo Anthony.

I remember one day in particular, when all 29 students begrudgingly moved at a glacial pace to the rug.

But not Elijah.

He was fast asleep. Face soft against the bean bag with, tented on his face, the Newbery words of Jackie Woodson.

There was a time in my career when I might have felt like it was an attack on me that a kid fell asleep in my class, and gotten upset with him. But that day, something told me to kneel down next to Elijah and ask him what was going on his world. It took all of one minute for Elijah to explain (with the help of his interjecting pal, Kalen) that he was having a hard day. He hadn't slept all night because he was handling some stress at home, he got kicked out of two classes before he even got to ours, and he hadn't eaten lunch because his recess had been revoked…because he was kicked out of two classes, probably because he hadn't slept. So goes the cycle.

I laid his favorite book back down on his face and told him to come over and join the class when he was ready.

More often than we know, we have kids entering our classrooms carrying some form of trauma beyond their control. Trauma induced by outside environments, adults in their school (yes, sometimes it's us), other kids in school, local or world events—they all take their toll. There is no socio-economic status, no gender, no race exempt from this. Mansions, name-brand clothing, and the latest technology aren't a shield.

Much of this can be invisible to us. It manifests in "loud," "angry," or "hyper" actions that get kids kicked out or moved down to red on behavior charts; leave them in tears in hallways and in class; get them into conflicts, into fights, into shootings.

Trauma does not have one face.

It's not a question of whether or not it was the right move to let a student sleep for an extra 15 minutes in my class that day. It's not very helpful to weigh whether it was right.

What is helpful? One minute. One book. One safe space.

That one minute I took to not just talk to, but listen to Elijah about his day gave me insight into his week, his year, and his identity. My hope is that at the end of that difficult day, when he got to my class, he finally felt heard.

Kids like Elijah and so many others have given me the greatest tools I have as a teacher: the value of maintaining a safe space flooded with reading material; time to read, to write, to wonder, to think, to be; and, at minimum, one minute of my best listening.

## Finding Time for Reading at Home

Children need to read at school, but they also need to read at home. Building a consistent reading routine at home challenges many families. Hectic afterschool schedules, transportation, caregivers' work demands, living space, book and library card access—there is a long list of factors contributing to inconsistent reading patterns at home. We need to do more to identify students' barriers to home reading. Do our students have quiet places to read? Do they own any books? What are their responsibilities after school? Don't just tell families that kids need to read at home— help them navigate the obstacles preventing reading at home from taking place.

Full disclosure: we struggle with maintaining consistent reading routines in our homes just like everyone else. Our families are busy with lots of evening and weekend activities. Ensuring that our kids are reading every night of their lives is a hassle— even for us. Honestly, there are a lot of distractions, and our reading motivation flags on a regular basis.

For many children, reading is a school job. If they do not build routines for reading at home, it is unlikely they will read much during the weekends, summer, or school breaks. Reading when it is not required of you shows that reading has personal value beyond school.

If we are realistic, reading time at home is always going to be a struggle to maintain. We don't commit to reading once. **We commit to reading each time we sit down and open a book.** There will be times when we can read at home, and times when we don't read much. Literacy thought leaders Kate Roberts and Maggie Beattie Roberts share their own struggle to maintain reading habits and provide wise advice for managing home reading lives.

## CHANGE IN ACTION

### Kate Roberts and Maggie Beattie Roberts
## Rebooting Reading

Take a moment and rustle up an old to-do list, an email to yourself of all the things to get done for the week, or perhaps a list of New Year's resolutions written way back when. What is something on that list you avoid doing? Is there anything in your life that you know you "should" do more, but when the time comes to face it, a part of you shrinks away? It sounds like, "I've got too much to do," or "It's just not the right time," or "I'll do this first thing tomorrow morning." We'll show you our list:

*Working out*
*Writing*
*Organizing*
*Meditating*
*Calling that company about that erroneous bill*

Notice something? Nearly everything on our list is really good for us. Not like normal, run-of-the-mill good for us. Nourishing good. Good for our lives, our bodies, and our spirits. (Well, except the one about calling that company…)

It is so easy to get bogged down in the mundane, surface-level activities of our lives. How can we not? The groceries need to be bought. The dinner needs to be cooked. The laundry has to get done, the car washed, the kids bathed. The job. The budget. The repairs and bills and phone calls. When we get a minute to ourselves, like many of you, we struggle to spend time on beneficial activities.

Instead, when we grab that free moment at the end of the day, we escape. And, the things we escape to are not exactly things that nourish us, like meditating. Here's our escape list:

*Watching TV*

*Laughing at things on the Internet*

*Yelling at things on the Internet*

*Sharing things on the Internet*

*Eating our sons' latest holiday stash of chocolate*

For many of you, reading books may be your favorite form of escape. You'll notice that we did not put reading on the top of our preferred end-of-the-day escape activities. Here is the truth: we struggle to choose reading over other escapes. It feels a little embarrassing, a little vulnerable to admit, but it is true.

And in this, we may be a lot like your students. Not the ones who devour every new book that enters your room, but the ones who need a reading reboot every time you see them. These are the kids who don't read at home or who aren't swayed by your modeling of a powerful, independent, and fun reading life. They just don't really want to read when they have the time.

We can empathize with them. Like ours, their lives are probably full of things to do: that assignment in social studies, cleaning their room, basketball practice, spending time with their family, processing their day. And when they do have the time, reading is not their go-to escape. Video games, YouTube, and Instagram are the escape places calling to them and providing relief after a long day. Perhaps those activities feel easier to them and don't require a lot of effort. They, like us, are wired to return to these activities habitually.

And yet, we know in our bones that reading is more like meditating and less like video games; more like exercise and less like escape. We know reading can be infinitely more rewarding and nourishing than scrolling through the Internet.

Here are some tips to help students rewire their experience with reading into the fulfilling, joyful one that we all know to be true:

## 1. FIND OUT WHY STUDENTS ARE RELUCTANT TO READ

We think we know our students. We spend so much time with them, how could we not? But we don't know them, at least not fully. We get a window into who they are in certain situations, but when we are confronted with a challenge like helping our kids read more, it always helps to do a little research.

That research can be tricky. Whenever we have asked "Why don't you like to read?" our students have responded with a shrug, often a bit confused themselves. Instead, let kids know that you noticed they don't love to read, and that this is normal, but you would like to explore why. Give them some choices of what the problem might be. Often giving choices to kids helps them see themselves in the answers (*Oooh, I'm that one!*). Instead of asking them to come up with the reason, you could say:

> *"I notice that reading isn't your favorite thing to do, is that right? You certainly aren't alone. Can I ask you—what is it about reading that doesn't grab you? Is it that it doesn't feel like it holds your attention? Do you not have the time and place to really get into a book? Or do you find reading difficult and so you don't feel like spending lots of time on it?"*

## 2. AFFIRM THEIR EXPERIENCE

It can be tough to be an avoidant reader in a classroom where the teacher is a super fan of books. We know that we alienated some kids when we talked at length about the love of reading and how it opens up new worlds. For many, this is a truth that is as real and natural as breathing. However, since it is not all of our kids' experience, we worry that we didn't give their reading identities and experience space in the room. Now we work to affirm what may repel some of our students from reading by getting their truth of reading resistance into the light. We say:

"I know! Reading can feel so boring at times. Sometimes unless I have the right book in my hands, I fall right to sleep when I read!"

Or, "When I have a lot to do or, am surrounded by my family I don't know how to get any reading done either. It never feels that high on my priority list."

Or, "When a book is tough, it kind of feels like the words are swirling around in my head. I kind of know most of what they mean, but they are not connecting and I feel lost."

### 3. SET SMALL READING GOALS TOGETHER

No amount of talk will launch most avoidant readers. But we can help our kids work on reasonable goals. Maybe your kids will read 10 minutes more that night than they did the night before. Maybe they will try to read two more books this year. Try setting goals that feel fair and doable.

"So let's think about tonight. How much time do you think you could read tonight? Five minutes while you wait for your brother to get picked up from school? That's awesome. I want you to do that, and then tomorrow we are going to have a high-five party about it, okay?"

### 4. NEVER GIVE UP

There will be that one kid who doesn't ever take to reading. Or the kid who does, and then slips back into avoiding reading once he's read that great series. Don't give up. The work isn't in the result, no matter what data heads say. It's in the process.

Keep working the four steps outlined here even when you and your kids are tired of it. You are planting seeds. And as you do that, have some sidekicks cheering you on and giving you language to help reach all readers. Some of our favorite teachers and mentor readers that help us shape these conversations with kids are Penny Kittle, Kelly Gallagher, Kristi Mraz, Pernille Ripp, and of course, Donalyn Miller and Colby Sharp. Whenever we hear their voices, they inspire us to keep tending to the garden of our own reading. They remind us, and our students, to continue gardening once the first seed is planted, or nothing will have the chance to grow.

## Stealing Reading Time

Yes, children need to read at school and home. But it is a rare reader—child or adult—who can set aside 30-minute chunks of reading time every day. Readers who keep their reading momentum going find ways to fit reading into the "edges" of their time (Miller, 2013). In order to find time to read, most readers steal it—10 minutes before bed, in the car on the way to soccer practice, while waiting at the bus stop.

Observing our students who read the most, we often see them stealing reading time. Breslin is reading his book out of his desk instead of listening to his teacher's writing mini-lesson. Sarah reads *Harry Potter and the Chamber of Secrets* while waiting for her mom's flat tire repair. When Ms. Haney comes to Colby's classroom door, Hailey pulls out her copy of *Wings of Fire #9: Talons of Power* to read while her teacher talks with the principal. Sneaky readers are everywhere: the kids who ignore morning announcements because they are reading, the children who walk through the halls reading a book—magically able to navigate crowded hallways without looking up, the adults who bring books to read everywhere they go in case of reading emergencies.

We can model and teach kids how to find small opportunities in their day to steal reading time. These small increments of reading snowball into a staggering amount of reading time. A child who steals 10 minutes of reading time a day racks up an incredible amount of reading over time. Reflecting on her childhood experiences with sneaky reading, teacher and instructional coach Kristin Ziemke describes how to help students identify moments when they could read by stealing reading time.

**CHANGE IN ACTION**

**Kristin Ziemke**

## Teach Sneaky Reading

I was a sneaky reader. I didn't have a name for it at the time, but that's what I was. I'd sneak a flashlight under my bed so I could read when I was supposed to be sleeping. I'd stash copies of The Baby-Sitters Club in my long-outgrown playhouse so I could stop by and squeeze in minutes with a book when I was supposed to be walking the dog. I'd even hide books under the bathroom sink before going to bed so I could get up a few moments later, feign a stomach ache, and spend some extra time with my favorite characters.

As a child, when I found a title that pulled on my heartstrings, I'd use every free moment I could find to get back into that book. Over the course of the day, those moments yielded 15 or 20 additional minutes with text. As an educator, I now recognize the impact sneaky reading had on my literacy development as those additional 20 minutes of daily reading provided me 1.8 million more words per year than my classmates who did not seek extra reading time (Nagy and Herman, 1987). I am a good reader because I read a lot.

*"The single greatest factor in reading achievement is volume."*

**—STEPHEN KRASHEN, *THE POWER OF READING***

Today I worry that too many of our students are not spending extensive time in text they can and want to read. There's increasing pressure on teachers

*Game Changer! Book Access for All Kids*

and families to prepare young learners for the "test du jour," often at the expense of quality reading. And as each year passes, there are more and more stakeholders who want "proof" that students are learning. As new technologies enter our classroom and the information age confronts us from all angles, it is critical that we teach students to be engaged, thoughtful readers so they can adapt to whatever learning conditions they find themselves in.

Instead of serving as testing factories, our schools need to be places where each child is provided explicit, personalized reading instruction. Schools must build enthusiasm for reading and celebrate favorite titles, introduce topics that pique children's interests, and support them in finding their next "home run" book. We need to use new and innovative tools like TheKidShouldSeeThis.com to view short video clips that spark curiosity and high-quality websites like Wonderopolis as a way to leverage technology to bring kids to text they want to read more about. But more than that, we must model how to live like a reader in our classrooms and beyond.

> *"A classroom atmosphere that promotes reading does not come from the furniture and its placement as much as it comes from the teacher's expectation that students will read."*
>
> **—DONALYN MILLER, *THE BOOK WHISPERER***

The need for highly proficient readers is urgent. I explicitly instruct my students in the art of sneaky reading. Together, we define what it means to be a sneaky reader and look for opportunities to practice our craft. Every morning we sneak minutes with books as students turn in lunch money, unpack their bags and settle in for the day. We leave morning work and bell-ringers behind and instead spend time with text. As we travel down the hall for bathroom break, our books go with us and we squeeze in a few more minutes of independent reading while we wait. Weekly we snuggle in for Flashlight Friday and lose ourselves in stacks of our favorite series and authors. On the bus to field trips, waiting for lunch cleanup, and when our schedule unexpectedly changes, we read. This becomes a habit not only at school, but a habit for living.

This practice extends beyond the school day as kids advocate for their reading life wherever they find themselves. Whether in line at the grocery store or cozying up with a book to quiet down after a busy day, extending a child's time with text creates the conditions in which thinking and learning never stops. We recognize that every minute counts, and as teachers we effectively use the time we have with students and actively seek ways to steal time we don't have. We teach students to be sneaky readers so they can independently carve out time to nurture their reading lives.

Looking to foster sneaky reading? Here are a few simple ways to embrace this practice with your students:

- Create a chart with students. Brainstorm all the moments throughout the day where students might "sneak" extra reading minutes.
- Share moments when you lived like a sneaky reader as a child.
- Document your life as a reader. Capture a book selfie on the train or ask a friend to snap a photo of you in a non-traditional reading environment. Model for your students when, where, and how to sneak additional reading minutes.
- Talk about the why. Give kids the facts regarding time with text and reading development.
- Flip your reading life! Use the ever-present power of technology to capture a video reading reflection or teaching point wherever you are to show how living like a reader transcends all aspects of your life.

# Closing Thoughts

We often hear complaints from other educators that kids have too many distractions preventing them from reading—video games, social media, watching videos on YouTube. It's more productive to consider why young people are willing to spend so much time on these activities. If kids aren't willing to dedicate time to reading or invest effort in learning to read well, we have to ask what's missing from their reading experiences that more enticing activities offer.

Instead of requiring kids to log minutes and pages on reading logs or take low-level comprehension tests on every book they read as an ineffective motivator, our students would be better served if we helped them connect with the books they want to read. The key to finding time to read isn't finding time at all. Kids will find time to read if they have something they want to read in the first place. Engagement and interest drive how much time you are willing to invest in reading.

See Donalyn and Colby discuss free choice for independent reading at scholastic.com/ GameChanger Resources

# The Power of Choice: Supporting Independent Readers

*"Any book that helps a child to form a habit of reading, to make reading one of his deep and continuing needs, is good for him."*
— MAYA ANGELOU

Lifelong readers have strong reading preferences and can self-select books successfully (Miller, 2013). When they visit a library or bookstore, they possess the knowledge and experience to preview and evaluate books and select books meeting their reading needs and interests. They didn't develop those abilities overnight— it took a lifetime of looking at books, making book choices, and reflecting on their reading experiences.

If we want children and teens to become lifelong readers, they need to practice and fine-tune their book-selection skills, too. Allowing them to choose the texts increases their reading motivation and interest (Gambrell, Palmer, Codling & Mazzoni, 1996; Worthy & McKool, 1996; Wigfield, et al., 2014). When children begin selecting their own books to read, many adults worry that they will make "inappropriate" book choices or select books that don't feed their reading development. Yes, many students struggle with making wise book choices. But we can help them by modeling how to preview and evaluate books and challenge themselves as readers.

Some educators question the importance of choice reading in the classroom. Burdened with curriculum demands, they feel that they do not have time to foster students' personal reading lives or that they lack school-community support for doing so. However, emphasizing academic reading over personal reading is shortsighted and undermines students' long-term literacy development. Self-selected reading is more powerful than teacher-selected reading in developing motivation and comprehension (Guthrie, et al., 2007). According to reading researcher Richard Allington, "It is during successful, independent reading practice that students consolidate their reading skills and strategies and come to own them. Without extensive reading practice, reading proficiency lags" (2014). Practice doesn't make perfect—practice makes permanent, and if we want students to internalize all of the knowledge and skills we teach them, we need to give them significant time to practice what they are learning in the context of real reading events.

Promoting students' personal ownership of reading ensures they will develop the literacy skills and attitudes about literacy they need to be successful now and in the future.

# The Benefits of Self-Selected Reading

When we give children and teens lots of opportunities to self-select books, we help them practice the skills and habits they need to become independent readers. When young readers choose what they read, it builds agency and confidence, and they are more likely to develop a positive orientation toward reading and stronger reading ability (Johnson & Blair, 2003). In this section, we discuss other benefits of giving children choices in what they read.

## Students Come to Value Their Decision-Making Process

We want children to develop the ability to make their own decisions. When they are young, we often frame choices in binary terms: make "good" choices instead of "bad" ones. We give them choices that require a simple a "yes" or "no" answer. Nuanced decision-making isn't so clear cut. We often consider several variables before making a choice such as where we might live or whether to accept a particular job. Giving children free choice sometimes doesn't mean we cede control of all decision-making to them; it should be an incremental process that becomes more complex with age and maturity (Taylor, 2009).

Encouraging young readers to select their own books from time to time fosters their autonomy and communicates your respect for their choices. When we consider the life-changing decisions children will face as they grow up, choosing a book offers a low-risk opportunity to practice sophisticated decision making.

## Students Learn to Choose Appropriate Reading Material

It takes time to learn strategies and develop book selection skills. The best way to nurture the process is to spend a lot of time with students looking at books, selecting books to read, reading them, and reflecting on the whole process. Urge them to ask themselves, "What appealed to me about this book in the first place? Was this a good book choice for me? Why or why not? Did this book provide what I was looking for this time? How did this book change me as a reader or person?" Children need lots of modeling, encouragement, and support to make wise book choices. No matter our personal reading preferences and opinions, we must celebrate whatever they choose to read and offer guidance when they have questions about books and their reading experiences.

Colby's student, Chandler, was committed to reading Gary Paulsen's *Hatchet*, even though it was too difficult for him to comprehend. Colby helped Chandler realize that the book was not the best choice for him now, but would be if he worked on building his reading skill. Chandler kept *Hatchet* in his desk and would pull it out every couple of months and try to read it. By the end of the year, Chandler was able to comprehend and enjoy *Hatchet*, and to gain reading confidence.

If Colby had forbidden Chandler from reading *Hatchet*, or shamed him for trying to read it, Chandler would have probably quit and decided he wasn't a good reader. Reading a book Chandler wanted to read was never a question; Colby always framed his discussions so that Chandler believed he would eventually be able to read not only *Hatchet*, but any book he wanted to read. There's a big difference between being unable to read a book right now and never being able to read it. Chandler's desire to build his skills until he could read *Hatchet* drove his interest in reading all year.

## Students Gain Confidence and a Feeling of Ownership

**Empowering children to select their own books feeds their self-esteem as readers and decision makers.** Conversely, when we restrict and control book choices, we discourage children from reading for their own purposes and to make their own decisions. Lifelong readers develop personal reading preferences and tastes over time, and discover reasons for reading that matter to them. It is unlikely that young readers will develop internal reading motivation if all their choices sit outside of them.

You can see confidence develop over a school year when children participate in nourishing, low-judgment reading communities that support and value their choices. At the beginning of the year, many students depend on their teachers or librarian for book recommendations because they don't have much experience choosing their own books, they don't see themselves as capable readers and therefore lack confidence, or they don't believe their teachers will approve of the books they choose. We have witnessed this metamorphosis from dependent reader to independent reader every year. With the right support, young readers can develop the confidence and experience they need to choose books for themselves long after leaving your class.

One of Donalyn's sixth graders, Katie, was reading at grade level, and Donalyn knew she was capable of reading books accessible to most sixth graders. So when

Katie told Donalyn that she wanted to read Beverly Cleary's *Ramona the Brave*, Donalyn didn't tell Katie that the book was too easy for her. Instead, she talked with Katie about why she chose the book in the first place. Katie said, "I know you told us we could read whatever we want, but I don't know what to read. I read this series in second grade and they were the last books I remember liking." Donalyn decided that Katie was overwhelmed with free choice, and needed lots of opportunities to preview books she might be interested in reading, as well as the chance to share and discuss books with other kids in class. With encouragement and practice choosing books, Katie's confidence grew over time.

## Students Become Better Test Takers

Children read more when they self-select their books. They stick with books longer and apply every reading strategy they know to navigate those books. Reading volume is the key to reading achievement (Krashen, 2004). If students don't read much, their reading test scores won't improve, no matter much we "prepare" them for those tests. The more children read and the more widely they read, the higher their test scores. Giving kids choice in what they read drives more reading and strong reading skills. Achievement is driven by interest.

## Students Become Lifelong Readers

We are more likely to engage in activities when we find them personally meaningful. When children choose their own books to read, they develop an attachment to reading and discover that reading is entertaining, edifying, comforting, and inspiring. The goal of all teaching is leading children to independence. What can we model and teach today that young readers can use for a lifetime? We often ask ourselves when evaluating a strategy, computer program, or activity, "Do readers really do this?" If the answer is no, why are we wasting time teaching it?

# What Choice Is and What It Isn't

Choice reading doesn't look the same from one school or classroom to the next. In some schools, children's choices are strictly limited and controlled. Students must select books from specific text level ranges, teacher-created lists, or district curriculum guides. Sometimes, educators prevent older students from reading illustrated texts, such as graphic novels and picture books, or series fiction because they aren't considered "rigorous" enough. Donalyn visited an elementary school where each child was told to select a book "at their level" for classroom work and a "dessert" book from the library for their own reading enjoyment, as if that reading was frivolous and without academic value. Whether we mean to or not, when we categorize texts in this way, we communicate to children that their personal reading interests aren't as important as our expectations for what and when they read. Too often, adults complain that kids don't read enough, then bemoan their reading choices when they do. We can't have it both ways.

Fourth-grade teacher Stacey Riedmiller has witnessed educators removing favorite books and series from their classroom libraries because students were reading them over and over instead of trying other books. Stacey recognizes that young readers often find comfort in and gain confidence from rereading books.

**CHANGE IN ACTION**

**Stacey Riedmiller**

# The Rewards of Rereading

*When children choose to reread a book series, they add dimensions to their understanding of that series.*

When children choose to revisit a book, they know the characters, they know the setting, and they know that everything will be all right in the end. This offers comfort, in a time when so many of our kids need comforting.

Last year, I had a reading conference with a student who was reading the Amulet series by Kazu Kibuishi for the second time. I asked him if he had found any new treasures this time around. His answer should bring joy to any educator's heart: "The first time I read through, I read with my brain. This time, I am reading with my heart." I understood just what he meant. If I had discouraged that child from rereading the series, and told him he needed to find something new, it would have been a missed opportunity.

Our responsibility is to encourage our students to read widely from different genres, eras, formats, topics, and perspectives. Offering children meaningful opportunities to choose, while ensuring they grow as readers, requires negotiation between academic and personal reading goals. **Readers' unique needs and interests should be the primary drivers of independent reading and matter more than mandates and expectations of teachers and caregivers.** If we want students to take ownership of reading, we have to give it to them—even when their book choices aren't successful or don't match our expectations.

## Guided Choice

Taking developing readers to the library and letting them pick whatever they want doesn't provide them with enough guidance, however. Many young readers do not know how to preview books and determine whether one is a good match for their abilities and interests. Don't presume that a fourth grader knows how to select a library book. Don't presume that an eighth grader knows. Some don't. According to the 2016 Scholastic Kids and Family Reading Report, 41 percent of the children surveyed reported that their parents and teachers underestimate how hard it is for them to find books to read. The more children select books and read lots of them, the easier finding books becomes: 57 percent of infrequent readers struggle with book selection, while only 26 percent of frequent readers do (Scholastic, 2016).

**Children need modeling and support from adults, and lots of opportunities to preview, share, and talk about books with their reading community peers, in order to become capable book selectors.** Unfortunately, the current nationwide focus on high-stakes testing leaves few opportunities for students to read self-selected books at school, which means they aren't getting much instruction or support on how to choose books.

So what's the middle ground between controlling book choice and giving children free rein? How can we teach and model authentic ways to choose books while honoring students' needs for self-determination and agency? It takes intentional focus and time, as well as rituals and routines.

## Rituals and Routines

Rituals and routines, the actions we habitually follow and behaviors we exhibit, can provide support, comfort, guidance, and ways of connecting with others. They reflect our cultural and personal beliefs and priorities. At the beginning of the school year, we teachers create learning rituals and routines in an effort to build successful learning communities. We structure them to reinforce our beliefs about literacy. We set the tone. We communicate the value system at work.

At a recent Scholastic National Reading Summit, Dr. Ernest Morrell described rituals through "temporal, spatial, and status" lenses (Morrell, 2017). In language arts classrooms, what do we make time for? What do we make space for? What do we give status to? What temporal, spatial, and status needs might we consider as we develop our rituals and routines?

## TIME

How do students spend their time in language arts class?

- What is the balance between teacher-directed instruction and student-directed inquiry and practice?
- Do children spend meaningful time every day reading, writing, and talking about topics of their own choice?
- Is there regular, dedicated time for reading aloud?
- How much time do we invest in family literacy education?

## SPACE

How do I organize our physical and intellectual spaces?

- Do we create spaces for students to share and discuss with one another what they're reading and writing?
- Does reading play a prominent visible role across our school?
- What are our curricular priorities?
- How do social justice, service learning, information literacy, critical thinking, and collaboration run through every subject?
- Do we create welcoming spaces for all families?

## STATUS

How do we decide what to emphasize or elevate?

- Do we budget for enough books and resources in libraries and classrooms?
- Do our institutional and instructional structures and behaviors perpetuate stereotypes and social/cultural inequities, or do they seek to dismantle them?
- Do we bestow privileges on certain students while withholding them from others?
- Do we celebrate and incorporate diversity throughout the school year, or only during holidays and designated months?
- Do we value students' test scores more than their reading lives?
- Do we value home literacy as much as school literacy?

The rituals and routines around reading that we implement at school and home, as well as our conversations about them, communicate what we value about reading and readers. What reading identities do our rituals and routines enforce? Are we leading our children toward healthy lifelong reading habits, empathy, and intellectual curiosity, or a life without books and reading?

Setting aside daily reading time is an important routine because it supports children's reading engagement and development. Providing regular opportunities for children to preview, share, and talk about books does, too.

# Book Talking and Book Pass

The rituals and routines we create to celebrate reading (and readers) should change from year to year in response to our students and their unique needs. Two practices we consistently use year after year are book talking and book passes, because they support and celebrate our students' reading engagement and effort.

## Book Talking

The only thing readers enjoy almost as much as reading is talking about books with other readers. Have you ever finished a book and felt compelled to put it in another reader's hands, with the plea, "I need you to read this book so that we can talk about it"? Creating a culture of reading at school and home includes lots of opportunities for young readers to share and talk about books with one another (Atwell & Merkel, 2016).

It's true that some readers prefer to invest more time in relationships with people inside their books than in face-to-face relationships with others, but discussions with other readers about books enhance reading lives.

When Donalyn began teaching, she assigned book reports to her students because all of the teachers on her team did. It didn't take Donalyn long to see how detrimental that was. Some of her students wouldn't read much until right before the book report was due. With the deadline looming, those students flew down to the library, picked out the shortest book they could find (*Sarah, Plain and Tall* at only 64 pages), skimmed the book or Googled it, wrote a passable report, then returned to not reading.

The goal of a book report is for students to prove to their teacher that they read a book, and we know kids can cobble together a book report without reading much. If all motivators for reading are external and punitive—and come from adults and are graded or evaluated—students' intrinsic motivation and their reading identity development fall by the wayside.

Recognizing the flaws of book reports, many educators have moved away from them in favor of book talks, short commercials about books. Book talks provide authentic persuasive speaking and writing opportunities by mirroring ways that readers share and recommend books to one another. The goal of a book talk is to convince other readers to read a book.

## Preparing for a Book Talk

Book talking begins with every adult in the school: teachers book talking in class, librarians book talking during library visits and school programs, administrators book talking during announcements or sharing book recommendations, as principals Brad, LaQuita, and Sue have described in this book. This creates a book-talking culture in the school.

Set aside two or three minutes each day to book talk a few books to your class. Allow book talks to happen spontaneously, too, when you are helping kids browse books in the school or classroom library. Book talks for groups of students should have broad appeal, while book talks for individual students should appeal to their individual abilities and interests. As former middle school teacher and children's author Kate Messner reminds us, "Book talking and individualized book recommendations are key to sustaining a classroom where every child is a reader" (Messner, 2016). Book talking builds relationships between and among readers.

Don't stress yourself out about book talking. It's not any different than sharing your thoughts about a favorite song or television show. Heartfelt testimonials work best. It doesn't have to be a production.

If you want to write some notes about the book in preparation, go ahead. But the best way to get ready for a book talk is to read the book. Your honest enthusiasm for it will inspire kids to read it. If you don't have time to read the book, research reviews and online resources and share them with students. Consider interesting ways to introduce the book. Share a book trailer. Connect the book to other books by the same author or in the same genre. Read an excerpt such as the first chapter, an exciting scene, a fascinating two-page spread from a nonfiction book, or a few poems. Colby struggled to find good examples of book talks on YouTube, so he decided to record at least one a week for his own channel.

## Encouraging Student-Led Book Talks

No matter our book-talking skill, the best readers to give students book recommendations are their peers. Who knows more about what seventh graders like to read more than another seventh grader? When we provide students with regular opportunities to recommend books, we foster reading relationships among our students that support them long after they leave our classrooms.

A month into the school year, Hailey came to class gushing about Gordon Korman's *Restart*. "Mr. Sharp, have you read this book? It is amazing. I stayed up super late last night, and I almost finished it."

"I have not read it yet. Thanks for the recommendation," Colby replied. The look Hailey gave him signaled that she was disappointed in him for not having read the book. She walked away without responding, sat down on one of our classroom couches, and began reading. Later, Colby was sitting on the carpet conferring with a student when he noticed Hailey talking to her friend, Reese. Colby couldn't hear what they were talking about, but at the end of their conversation, Reese took *Restart* and put it in her book box.

The following Monday, Reese asked Colby if she could give a book talk during their regular book-talking time—snack break. Then Colby asked Reese what book she wanted to talk, to which she replied, "I read this amazing book called *Restart* over the weekend. Kids in this class are going to love it. Have you read it?" Colby shook his head and smiled.

Reese gave an amazing book talk that morning, and a few kids added *Restart* to their to-read list. Reese passed the book to Russell, and Russell finished the book later that week.

Months later, with only a handful of days left in the school year, Tobin came up to Colby and told him that the previous night he got his very own library card. Colby had been talking a lot in class about ways to get books during the summer, and a bunch of his students expressed interest in getting library cards. Colby was so excited for Tobin. They talked about the card-acquisition process, the library itself, and the books Tobin had checked out, including *Restart*. Tobin said he knew other kids had been talking about it, so it was probably a book he would enjoy reading.

You can find abundant book-talking resources online, or you and your students can record your own book talks and share them with readers year to year. We see all sorts of creative ways to celebrate and share books that include students' voices, such as posting book talks on Flipgrid and/or Padlet, or recording them for a school news show.

Book talking supports readers in the moment and down the road. Students celebrate books they've enjoyed while earmarking books they might read next. Book talking honors their voices, recognizes their reading experiences and preferences, and keeps their reading momentum going.

## Book Pass

Have you ever felt certain books in your classroom or library were not receiving the love they deserve? Have you ever wondered why students ignore an amazing book? Have you ever struggled to add a bunch of new books to your classroom library all at once? Do your students overlook incredible books and series because they aren't new? Giving students regular opportunities to preview books they might miss can spark interest in reading them and expand students' reading choices and book knowledge.

Book pass (Allen, 2000), speed dating with books, book tastings… no matter what you call it, the process is similar. Teachers and librarians collect stacks of books they think their students might be interested in reading. Those books might include titles for units of study in science and social studies, genres students don't read enough, authors with high appeal, new books, older books—any books you think would enrich students' reading experiences. Determine your goals when selecting books and work with colleagues and your librarian to find as many as possible.

### Preparing for a Book Pass

There are different ways to manage book passes, but the basic sequence remains the same. You begin by stacking books on tables or stations around your room or library. Be sure to offer many books for each student. You can organize students into groups randomly or by reading interests or goals. Then invite students to spend a few minutes looking at the books—reading the blurb on the back cover or jacket flap, browsing the illustrations, and/or sampling a few pages. Ask students to record any titles that interest them on their to-read lists in their reader's notebooks. After the book pass, create reserve lists for any hot titles and let students check out books. Reunite as a group to celebrate and share the books you have discovered.

Colby stacks 20 to 50 books in different stations around his classroom, and students travel from station to station, previewing books at each station for 6 to 10

## Book Pass Basics

1. Select books.
2. Place books at each book pass station.
3. Organize students into groups.
4. Model how to preview a book and record entries on a to-read list.
5. Give students a set time to travel through each book pass station.
6. As a group, share titles students are excited to read.

minutes. When Colby calls time, he encourages students to select one or two books they want to read immediately and take them to the next station.

After students have made it through all of the stations, Colby encourages students who haven't found a book to revisit stations. Once everyone has found books to add to their to-read lists and book boxes, the class gathers in the meeting area and shares some of the titles they discovered.

Donalyn organizes book passes differently, shortening the time students spend looking at each book before passing on it and creating hold lists for high-demand books, but her goals and results are the same as Colby's.

Our best advice: keep moving; don't spend too much time looking at the same stack of books; include as many voices, genres, and formats in stacks as possible; and figure out how to fairly distribute books that seem the most popular with kids. No matter how you organize your book pass, don't lose sight of your purpose for doing it: to introduce students to a host of books they might read and to encourage conversations between and among students about books.

## When You Need a Book Pass

Try a book pass when you feel your students need more exposure to books they might read:

### Before a school break

Hosting a book pass before breaks sends the message that school vacations offer opportunities for students to read books of their choice. To increase motivation and ensure access, browse books with students and select some to read over the break, then send them home with those books.

### When kids are reading the same books over and over

We love it when students fall in love with a series, author, or genre. There is nothing like watching a child devour the entire Harry Potter series or discover Jason Reynolds and read all of his books. However sometimes those children struggle to jump into other series, authors, and genres, and their reading motivation and enthusiasm flags.

Readers benefit from taking a break from reading a large series or reading one author or genre at the exclusion of others. Colby's student Reese enthusiastically read the first five books in Tui T. Sutherland's Wings of Fire series, but lost her reading steam halfway through book six. During a book pass, she discovered Lauren Wolk's *Wolf Hollow* and read it over Thanksgiving break. When school resumed, Reese declared, "*Wolf Hollow* is the best book I've read all year," and pleaded for everyone to read it. Then she jumped back into the Wings of Fire series with renewed energy.

### When new books are added to the classroom library

While we try to book talk individual new books before adding them to our classroom libraries throughout the year, there are moments when we want students to look at a lot of new books at once. Book passes provide opportunities to explore many titles in one sitting.

Each year Colby's school district budgets $250 for teachers to spend on their classroom libraries. Because Colby always wants to use the money strategically, he waits until he gets to know his students each year before spending it. He wants the books he purchases to reflect his students' interests and needs, and fill any gaps in his collection. Giving students a chance to preview new books before classmates begin checking them out helps students keep track of the ones they want to read, before they disappear from the library.

### When old favorites are being overlooked

The popularity of certain books changes from one year to the next. This year, you have a lot of soccer players and Star Wars fans; next year, everyone wants to read about dragons or World War II. Books that fly off the shelves one year can gather dust the next. Book passes are great ways to get some old favorites in front of new readers.

### To introduce kids to authors they don't know

Don't assume children know much about authors who write books for them. Colby was shocked to discover early one year that none of his fourth graders had read a Beverly

Cleary book. So he dedicated an entire station to Cleary books during a book pass, and the Ramona books and *The Mouse and the Motorcycle* became popular reads. Bring in additional books by authors kids meet through read-alouds or units of study. When kids find authors they like, it almost always sparks a desire to read more.

### To introduce kids to genres and formats they aren't reading

When children avoid certain genres or formats, we assume they haven't had positive, engaging experiences reading them (Miller, 2013). What books do students avoid reading or claim they dislike? Book passes give students time to preview and choose books they might not approach on their own. Colby struggled to encourage his students to read poetry. Adding multiple copies of Kwame Alexander's *The Crossover* and *Booked* to a book pass station changed his students' perceptions of poetry, and those books got passed from one student to the next.

# How Do We Find a Book to Read?

Concerned that her middle schoolers often struggled with choosing library books, Donalyn worked with them to identify the book selection skills they needed.

Upon returning to the classroom from a weekly library visit, Donalyn gave students a few minutes to share the books they just checked out. "I know everyone is excited about the new books you found today. I am curious. How did you decide that book was the book you were checking out today? How did you discover it? How did you know it was a good book for you?"

Students chatted with their table partners for a few minutes, then Donalyn invited students to share how they selected their library books. Alex said, "I got the next Amulet, the sixth one. I have already read the rest of the series, and I cannot wait to read this one!" He held the graphic novel over his head for emphasis, sparking cheers from several classmates who enjoyed this fantasy series, too.

Donalyn started a list on the whiteboard titled, "Ways to Find a Book to Read" and wrote "series" next to the first bullet. "How many of you picked your book today because it's part of a series you enjoy?" Several hands shot up.

Next, Destiny shared that she checked out a nonfiction book on dogs she hadn't read. Hailey chose *Ghetto Cowboy* by Greg Neri, another book from that year's Bluebonnet Award reading list. She planned to read all 20 books on the list. Heavenly checked out *One for the Murphys* by Lynda Mullaly Hunt because several of her friends told her it was "amazing." Riley admitted that she picked a short book because she had a lot of soccer games that week, while Skylar selected a long fantasy book because she knew she was going on a road trip to her grandmother's house in Austin and needed something to read in the car so she, in her words, "wouldn't have to look at cows out the window the whole time!"

Donalyn added "topic," "book list," "length," and "recommendations" to the class-created list. Then everyone spent a few minutes discussing the people who gave them book suggestions—teachers, librarian, friends, family members, and so on. Finally, Donalyn invited each child to show off his or her book and describe how it was chosen. In a few minutes, Donalyn and her students had generated this list:

- Series
- Format (graphic novels, short stories, books of lists, etc.)
- Cover (We joke about not choosing a book by its cover, but we do.)
- Topic
- Award or Book List
- Reviews
- To-Read List
- Recommendations
- Read the blurb
- Read a few pages
- Skim the table of contents or visuals
- Length

After celebrating everyone's book choices, Donalyn invited her students to try a new method for choosing a book the next time they needed one. "If you chose a book today because the cover looked interesting, next time, get a recommendation from a friend or open the book and read a few pages. Think about different ways to look at books to decide if they look good to you." Over time, students built greater capacity to evaluate books and identify ones they would like to read.

Introducing students to different formats or platforms such as ebooks and audiobooks can increase their reading engagement and interest. Antero Garcia shares his experiences using audiobooks and multimodal texts in written, oral, and visual formats to entice adolescents to read more. Respecting students' reading choices includes honoring how they access texts. All reading counts in an inclusive reading community!

**CHANGE IN ACTION**

**Antero Garcia**

## Audiobooks, Interactive Media, and What Counts as Reading

To make a class novel more accessible to all of my students one year, I installed an unabridged audiobook version of it on all of their digital devices. Some students complained that listening to a book is "boring," so Solomon, a serious-mannered classmate, stated, "You just gotta listen. You can't do anything else." He then paused before concluding, "It's like reading."

I've spent a lot of time reflecting on Solomon's words and reimagining what "counts" when it comes to cultivating passionate readers. Throughout the remainder of that school year, students often used earphones during silent reading time. Audiobooks were appreciated side-by-side with traditional print-based novels, comic books, manga, and magazines in the classroom.

That isn't to say letting Solomon and his classmates use their headphones went perfectly. The tinny warble of music spewing from headphones sometimes distracted classmates, and we observed students swiping and tapping on video games. Some students were *not* listening to audiobooks, in other words. However, these incidents point to two tensions that can emerge when teachers broaden what "counts" as reading in our classrooms:

1. Multimodal reading of text doesn't look like the reading that teachers are used to assessing and supporting.
2. Using digital resources in classrooms requires trust between teachers and students.

Though we have miles to go, we are getting closer to a more robust understanding of "reading"; even textbook companies are savvy enough to begin packaging multimodal resources with the books. At the same time, I recognize that there are cognitive differences between reading with your eyes, listening to the same text, and watching an interactive story come into being through a gaming console. However, these differences must be reconciled with meaningful expectations of comprehension. Just as I was able to see many of my students discover the joys of reading by encouraging them to read comic books, Solomon reminds us that there are myriad students who may be itching to become active and joyful readers if we encourage them to plug into texts in different ways.

At the same time, trust between students and teacher is important. Allowing students to listen privately—something that teachers may not be able to monitor—means reimagining how texts, students, and teachers interact. If we're taking an honest look at classrooms today, we must acknowledge the frequent cat-and-mouse game of teachers "catching" students in the act of texting, playing, or otherwise being distracted by their phones. As we reimagine the role of technology in the lives of young readers, we must also reimagine what trust *means* around that technology as well. How I consume media today looks vastly different than it did when I was in school. I still have a pile of books next to my bedside that I work through ever so slowly, and some of these books are queued up on a Kindle rather than in physical form. I spend a lot of time listening to audiobooks and podcasts. I have also spent a lot of time studying and playing interactive fiction and games that offer narrative fulfillment. In other words, what "counts" as reading in my own life looks very different from when I was younger.

As technology continues to find its way into classrooms today, we must consider the modalities of reading we are willing to include. More importantly, we must consider what opportunities are denied, and what interests are diffused, when we *exclude* certain kinds of media.

# Closing Thoughts

Supporting young readers in self-selecting their own books requires explicit modeling and teaching in how to locate, preview, and evaluate books. Children need lots of support and encouragement for their reading choices. Independent readers can successfully choose books based on their interests and reading experiences. Most of all, choice is empowering and helps young readers develop confidence.

# Our Community of Readers: The Relationships Readers Need Every Day

See Donalyn and Colby discuss the importance of creating a community of readers at scholastic.com/GameChanger Resources

*"If no one close to you takes joy in reading, where is the evidence that it's worth the effort?"*

**—CARL SAGAN**

Throughout this book, we have emphasized the responsibility educators, families, and community members hold for ensuring that all children and adolescents have meaningful access to books and the opportunity to fall in love with reading through positive reading experiences at school and home.

Let's be clear: It is going to take all of us. A sustained, organized, and unwavering commitment to these goals will be the only way we can change the institutional and social structures preventing young readers from receiving the book access, expert instruction, and home support they need. In spite of significant obstacles, many communities have found solutions that work.

In every chapter thus far, we have provided research, resources, our thinking, and testimonials from educators, parents and caregivers, and community leaders. Based on decades of research and work in schools, we can identify the actions that foster strong reading communities:

- Create a sense of urgency to motivate change at school and home.

- Increase the number and variety of books in libraries, classrooms, and student homes.
- Increase children's interactions with books through independent reading and read-alouds.
- Help students develop strong rituals and routines for independent reading.
- Encourage students to listen, speak, and write about their reading.
- Model a literate life.

In this final chapter, we feature seven individuals and groups who have found powerful methods for building reading communities in their classrooms, libraries, homes, and across the United States. Their suggestions, beliefs, and experiences provide you with more resources, validation, and inspiration for the work ahead. **We can change the world for kids. It is possible.** We celebrate all of you who are committed every day to this transformative work.

Kyle Zimmer, President, CEO and co-founder of First Book, a nonprofit organization that works to connect schools and publishers to provide low-cost books to schools in need, shares the origins of First Book and the resources they provide that can support your community.

### CHANGE IN ACTION

**Kyle Zimmer**

## Overcoming Inequity One Book at a Time

*First Book believes that education is a child's best path out of poverty.*

Our mission is simple and powerful: to provide all children equal access to a quality education by making books and other resources available to classrooms and programs serving kids in need, from birth to age 18. Any educator or program leader who serves children from low-income households can register with us, free of charge.

First, we provide only the highest quality, *brand-new* books and educational resources. We know firsthand that receiving something completely brand-new has an outsized effect on a child living in poverty—and on their teachers.

Second, we work directly with the dedicated and formidable educators serving millions of kids from low-income families. Our book and resource inventory is shaped by their feedback and remains relevant to the children they serve.

Third, we are a nonprofit social enterprise. We leverage proven e-commerce strategies to apply a sustainable, market-driven model to the problem of affordability and access to books and resources. Every purchase from First Book supports a solution to educational inequity and makes a difference in the lives of children in need. The First Book Network is made up of hundreds of thousands of registered educators who are part of the estimated 1.3 million U.S. classrooms and programs in low-income communities. Our network grows by 1,000 additional members each week, making First Book the largest and fastest-growing network of educators serving children in need.

Anyone who works with a classroom or program in which a minimum of 70 percent of the children served are from low-income homes is eligible for First Book resources. Our network includes formal and informal educators from a range of settings, including Title I schools, nationally-known education programs, local libraries, museums, preschool and after-school programs, homeless shelters, faith-based programs, health clinics, juvenile justice programs, summer meal sites, and more.

First Book has grown into an award-winning nonprofit social enterprise that now reaches more than five million children annually—children who might not otherwise know the power of books in their lives. As of this writing, we have distributed more than 175 million books over more than 25 years, and we hear almost every day that, for many children, the books they receive from First Book are the only books they own.

By investing in the educational opportunities for children growing up in low-income families, we can change the trajectory for individual children and for society. And the most hopeful understanding is this: We can do this together.

And you can start right now. To learn how to become a First Book member, please see scholastic.com/GameChangerResources.

Project LIT is a national, grassroots literacy movement and growing network of dedicated teachers and students who work together to increase access to culturally relevant books and promote a love of reading in our schools and communities. Project LIT founder Jarred Amato describes the origins of Project LIT, their goals, and how educators can involve their students and colleagues in the project.

**CHANGE IN ACTION**

**Jarred Amato**

# The Project LIT Community

I still remember *The Atlantic* headline "Where Books Are All But Nonexistent." As I scrolled through the article, which described the effects of growing up in a "book desert," I immediately thought of my high school students and our East Nashville community and its limited book access.

I spent the rest of the summer developing an introductory unit for my sophomores. Three weeks later, we read the article together. I prepared a few questions to get us started, but intentionally left the answers up to them:

- What are book deserts?
- Why are book deserts harmful?
- Why do you think book deserts exist?
- What can we do this year to solve this problem?
- What ideas or suggestions do you have?

From that lively first discussion, Project LIT Community was born, and over the past two years, our passionate, persistent students have turned a class project into a nationwide movement, one step and one book at a time.

While our organization now includes more than 250 schools, or chapters, across the country, our goal remains the same: to increase book access and to promote a love of reading, so that all children become lifelong readers.

We soon realized that our goal was more than increasing book access— it was to increase access to high quality, culturally relevant books—books that invite all students to see themselves in the pages. Books that affirm our students' identity and culture. Books that communicate to all students that their voices, their stories, and their lives matter. Books that spark necessary conversations in our classrooms and community. Books that help promote empathy and kindness. Books that encourage children to fall in love with reading again or for the first time. Books that encourage students to write stories of their own. Books that make us laugh and cry and think differently about the world and our place in it.

Next, we started Project LIT Book Club. Our first pick was already a class favorite: *The Crossover* by Kwame Alexander. We've hosted a book club every month since: *March: Book One, Ghost, Booked, All American Boys, The Hate U Give, A Long Walk to Water, Solo, Dear Martin, March: Book Two, Long Way Down,* and *The Poet X.* Of course, Project LIT Book Club is about celebrating and discussing great books, but it is also about creating a sense of belonging.

While our students have grown as readers (there is plenty of positive peer pressure to finish the book each month), they have grown even more as leaders. Our students run every aspect of the event. To prepare for the book club, our students develop all of the discussion questions, create poetry and artwork inspired by the novels, design graphics, craft Twitter posts, and send email invitations to community members.

On the day of the book club, our students sign guests in, prepare speeches, facilitate small-group discussions, update our Instagram story, and host our trivia competition. Following the event, they reflect on the experience, write thank-you letters, and begin to generate excitement for the next book club selection. Beyond the monthly book club, our students are true reading role models for our community. We wrapped and delivered books to local elementary schools before the holidays and have taken advantage of every opportunity to speak to others about the importance of literacy. We have also partnered with local organizations to bring best-selling authors Kwame Alexander, Jason Reynolds, and Nic Stone to Nashville.

We recently announced our 12 middle grade and 13 young adult titles that will serve as the official Project LIT Book Club selections for the 2018–19 school year. These books will bring together students and teachers from the Bronx to Los Angeles, and hundreds of communities in between. To learn how to lead your own LitProject, please see scholastic.com/GameChangerResources.

Literacy specialist Valinda Kimmel has worked as both a literacy coach supporting teachers' instruction and an intervention teacher. Mr. Duke is one of the teachers at her Title I campus. In the beginning, many of his students were unmotivated readers and lacked the confidence and skills needed to become strong, engaged readers.

**CHANGE IN ACTION**

**Valinda Kimmel**

# Nurturing Reading Student Identities

*"I'm not a very fast reader. Well … I'm not a very good reader. I don't want to pick a hard chapter book because I won't finish it. I've never finished a book like that by myself before. Ever."*
**—MAKENZY, FIFTH GRADER**

Kids enter classrooms every day knowing who they are as readers. Their understanding of themselves as readers may be confirmed, challenged, or changed depending on their classroom experience. Teachers have the responsibility and privilege to cultivate a space that nurtures an affirmative identity for readers.

In literacy development, identity matters (McCarthey & Moje, 2002; Moje, et al., 2009). Studies show that students' reader identities connect in intricate ways with their reading practices inside and outside of the classroom. And students present identities for particular contexts (Gee, 2000). "People tell others who they are, but even more important, they tell themselves and then try to act as though they are who they say they are" (Holland, Lachicotte, Skinner, & Cain, 1998).

Teachers see this multiplicity every day. Some students believe they can't read well like their peers; others say they're accomplished readers yet never finish a book or talk about what they plan to read next. Still others identify themselves as slow readers and have a fluency rate well below grade level, but can have meaningful discussions about what they read. Students also get a clear idea of who they are as readers by their placement in special programs or intervention groups—and it's not always positive.

What does it take to facilitate the formation of a healthy, authentic reader identity? Kids need to:

- Read books they've chosen for themselves.
- Talk about books.
- Journal about their emerging ideas and understandings about texts.
- Have a plan for what they'll read next.
- Speak from experience about the application of strategies for comprehending texts.
- Choose to read from a variety of genres, types, and media.
- Challenge their own and others' observations about author's craft.
- Listen respectfully to peers as they discuss texts and disagree graciously when needed.
- Change the way they think and feel in some aspect of their lives or take action due to the transforming power of great texts.

Across our country and beyond, wise and wonderful teachers understand how to help shape these dynamic reader identities.

I know such a teacher.

Mr. Duke helps guide a flourishing community of readers in his fifth-grade classroom. He starts a new book study cycle with his students by using compelling text excerpts to teach, model, or revisit strategies for deep understanding. The short text selections come from the books he's making available to students for that round of book clubs—a preview, if you will. Excitement grows. Kids talk about the excerpts, make predictions, and chat about which books they'll read.

Kids prioritize their choices, and Mr. Duke matches books to kids. Students spend 20 to 25 minutes each day reading and making notes in their journals. They're encouraged to find evidence of developing themes from the collection of books for this round: perseverance, loyalty, or isolation. Posters around the room show ways to infer, ask questions, or make connections within and across texts and include sentence starters for students who aren't sure what to write.

To initiate group discussion, Mr. Duke shares highlights from the previous day—citing examples of conversations he heard around the room, discussions that included journal notes, and purposeful use of textual evidence. Next, he reads from sticky notes he took from a chart titled *Evidence of Great Discussions*. Students fill this chart with one another's thoughts—quotes they've captured during group discussion. Mr. Duke mentions by name the student who wrote the note and the student who shared the original observation.

You can imagine these few minutes in the reading block are powerful. Students are recognized for listening well to their peers and acknowledged for thinking about and articulating what they are reading. And in the process, students are watching Mr. Duke model how readers talk insightfully about texts.

Next, students break into groups for discussion. They share journal entries, point to text selections, and discuss themes, plot twists, or sudden changes in characters. All the while, Mr. Duke listens, occasionally joining the conversation for support.

Group discussions include students at every level: advanced readers alongside their peers who receive SPED (special education) services, reading intervention, behavioral assistance, and ESL support.

Every last one of them is a reader with something to contribute to the reading community in their classroom.

Of course, this doesn't happen by accident. Mr. Duke designed this environment: he created structures and blocked out time, chose texts accessible to all students through audio versions or visiting readers, and modeled for his learning community what it means to be a reader.

> *"Since we got back from the holiday break, I've read three chapter books. That's more books than I think I read all last year. I'm going to read another book by the author who wrote* The Honest Truth. *Did you know he wrote more books? I like his books."*
>
> **—KEVIN, FIFTH GRADER**

Mr. Duke "tells his students who they are, but even more important they tell themselves and then try to act as though they are who they say they are" (Holland, et al.).

We must create literary communities that "tell" kids who they are so they can develop habits and dispositions that establish their identity as a reader. An identity that will serve them now and well into adulthood.

Middle school teacher Katherine Sokolowski describes the importance of classroom libraries in building a reading community for her students in a small, rural town. Her students see her classroom as a refuge where their voices and choices matter.

**CHANGE IN ACTION**

### Katherine Sokolowski

# Book Refuge

What I know to be true is that if children are surrounded by books that look interesting to them, they will pick them up. If they pick them up, there is a good chance they will read them. If they read them and enjoy them, there is a good chance they might repeat the process again. Thus, my students are surrounded by books.

In our small rural farming community of approximately 5,000, the nearest bookstore is 30 miles away. Beyond the classroom library, my students have access to our school library and a public library in town. The majority of my students are middle class, but my 75 seventh graders reflect the economic spectrum. We have students who are the first born American citizens in their family, and students who are the children of professors at the university a few towns over. We have students who never have to worry about their next meal, and students who are homeless. For a variety of reasons, just over half of my students have a public library card. Less than half have purchased books online or in bookstores. Several named the Scholastic Book Fairs, which we hold twice a year, as the only place they've bought a book. Almost all mentioned at least one book of their own at home, a third had 10 or less. They all have access to books because of our libraries at school, but without the school and classroom library, some would be without a single book.

My student Estella recently wrote about the impact of having books when we discussed access and book deserts. "I remember what it was like to run out of books over spring break. I don't know what I would do if I had no books at all.

Books are my refuge." Books are the refuge for many of our students, as they were for me as a kid, and still are. When I told my students that I was writing this piece, I mentioned that I felt our library was the heart of the classroom. Ian immediately piped up and said, "No, not the heart, the lifeblood. We cannot survive without it." Access to books is essential. It changes the trajectory for many kids. I cannot imagine my classroom without books and am glad I never have to.

High school reading intervention specialist Anna Osborn knows that it's never too late to engage a student with reading or build positive relationships with students. Anna shares her experiences with one student, Amad, and the place she helped him find for himself in books and in the classroom community.

**CHANGE IN ACTION**

**Anna Osborn**

## A Matter of Belonging

"Amad doesn't belong in my class," I told my principal, echoing other students in my reading intervention classes. Before I met Amad, I would try to convince these students—identified as needing extra literacy support because they scored two or more years below grade level on state and district tests— of the benefits of taking reading class. "Mrs. Osborn," one would interject, "I don't belong in reading. I read fine. I just don't like it." I came to realize these objections were a pride-saving reaction to the perceived stigma of being in a reading class. Although Amad didn't voice objections, I knew he challenged my skill and training.

I had a difficult time identifying the kind of instruction Amad, a 15-year-old Somali teen, needed. He was an accomplished copier. He strategically partnered with others, and, whenever my questions brought me closer to identifying his needs, Amad disrupted class. New to teaching emerging bilinguals, I could barely untangle reading issues from language issues.

I realized I had reached a crossroads in my career. I could either identify students who didn't belong in my reading class, or I could teach all of the students in my reading class. I advocated for Amad's needs while district red tape bounced his file from special education to the ELL department. Oblivious to behind-the-scenes happenings, Amad could not wait for specialists to decide his fate. Instead, he gave me my answer: I teach all of the students in my class.

In a lesson where my ELLs made CDs of picture books for our elementary partners, I stepped toward my changing view. I acknowledged the difficulty of the job I asked Amad to do. "Reading is hard work," I reassured him. "I will teach you." Circulating during practice time, I stopped by Amad's desk several times to read with him. My change became his change. After this, as though sensing he belonged to our classroom community of readers, Amad began to take academic risks.

Amad seldom comes to class simply to copy notes anymore. Recently, he came in during study hall to complete a wish list of soccer books for our upcoming field trip. "Is this the author?" he asked, pointing to a subtitle on his computer screen. As I showed how he could find the author's name, I marveled that Amad did something none of his classmates were able to do: he generated a list of books about popular soccer stars that fell within budget.

Some days are not so smooth. Like many teens, when he's tired, after I tell him to choose something to read, Amad will respond, "Aw, c'mon, Mrs. Osborn." But I simply grab a selection of titles from the shelf and pull my chair up next to him. I learned my lesson. Amad belongs in my class.

While Colby understands the importance of school librarians, he has never worked in a school with a certified librarian. In the following essay, Colby describes how working with librarian Margie Culver helped him grow as a teacher. Thanks to her guidance, he now creates new reading community opportunities and experiences for his fifth-grade students.

## LIBRARIANS MAKE A DIFFERENCE

I have never worked in a school with a certified librarian. It wasn't until I got active on Twitter in 2011 that I even realized many schools had certified librarians. The more time I spent learning from amazing librarians online, the more I realized that my students were really missing out. The students in schools with certified librarians were frequently Skyping with authors, they had libraries filled with the latest and greatest books for kids, and they were celebrating different book holidays (Poem In Your Pocket Day, World Read Aloud Day, Read Across America Day). I implemented the ideas I learned from school librarians to make sure my students didn't miss out on these amazing opportunities.

Margie Culver, one of the school librarians from whom I learned the most, was doing such exciting things with her students in Charlevoix. It was easy to see that her passion for children's literature was rubbing off on her students. After retiring, Margie started volunteering in my classroom once a week. She would bring books to read aloud, books to book talk, and a story-telling lamp. Instantly, the kids fell in love with her. As she got to know my students, the books she brought in to book talk would be tailored to books that she thought individual students might enjoy. Every book she brought in became a hit with my readers. There is no substitute for having certified librarians in our schools. Watching Margie with young readers was a thing of beauty.

As the library coordinator for a suburban school district, Becky Calzada spends her days supporting the librarians in her district as they work to build strong reading communities in their schools. As a grandmother, Becky reads and shares books with her grandchildren and emphasizes the role that all family members can take in fostering a love of reading with the children in their lives.

**CHANGE IN ACTION**

**Becky Calzada**

# Creating a Family Reading Life

Some of my most cherished moments revolve around reading with my children and, now, with my grandchildren. For many reasons, our multigenerational home is saturated with books for readers of all ages. Yes, I'm a teacher-librarian and know the importance of reading—and so, too, does the American Academy of Pediatricians. On every well-check for children, the AAP encourages parents to read aloud daily beginning at birth (CECP, 2014)!

So why read to kids? For me, it's about being a reading role model. When I was raising my two daughters, I wanted them to see how important reading was in both their school and personal life. Now, I want my grandkids to know that reading is fun. It teaches us about our world and creates memories of the special times we share with books. This time also affords us the opportunity to talk about the characters in the books we read, predict what will happen, or wonder why certain characters behave the way they do. All these conversations lay the foundations  for being better prepared for school and build vocabulary skills that prepare readers to become better listeners and writers, too.

We're also building reading traditions. We read nightly, but I've begun additional reading traditions with my grandkids and other readers I know, both old and young, such as giving books for birthdays and holidays. For these special occasions, I carefully select titles I think family and friends will enjoy, and I write a small note inside the book with the date and year. In our home, these titles become part of holiday traditions where we take out all the "Easter books," "Halloween titles," and

"Christmas titles." Reflecting on past years' purchases provides a trip down Memory Lane and also creates a reading timeline for each child.

In *The Power of Moments*, authors Chip and Dan Heath share that moments of connection "are strengthened because we share them with others" (2017). Books can be the connectors that bring families together. Reading about what happens in the world via books can launch amazing conversations between children and adults. Sharing beloved books will trigger fond memories and also give your child insight into your reading life. What a literacy legacy to leave behind!

As much as we try to shelter children from the harsh realities of our world, we do them a disservice when we avoid tough topics such as poverty, violence, family issues, and prejudices that many of our children suffer every day. This trauma affects not only students' academic potential, but their ability to grow into resilient, capable adults. Kindergarten teacher Aeriale Johnson invites us into her classroom and shows how love, powerful conversations, and books give her young students the tools they need to navigate the world.

**CHANGE IN ACTION**

**Aeriale Johnson**

# The Bearable Heaviness of Reading

*"Reading is better than food."* —**MY STUDENT, AGE SIX**

As I knelt to confer with a kindergartener, she described the place where she goes to visit her father. She never said so, but the details she painted with her words revealed the inside of a prison. "I go there in a pattern," she said. "See my dad. Don't see him. See my dad. Don't see him." We had been working on finding patterns to help us tackle books during guided reading. She had mastered that skill and was clearly transferring it to develop a more important theory.

Every school day, beautiful, tiny human beings walk into our building, toting backpacks and baggage. They stuff their backpacks into too-small cubby holes in the entryway, but the baggage comes with them into our classroom. Teaching children who experience trauma is challenging work. The social worker on our campus warns me to practice self-care lest I experience compassion fatigue. And I do. The moment I leave school each day, I begin reading.

Ever since Sylvia Plath, ironically, saved my life through *The Bell Jar* in my late teens, I have clung to books. Through the inevitable seasons, bibliotherapy has been the force that gives my life meaning. Books help us forge connections to ourselves and to each other. These connections heal us from traumatic experiences and release us to initiate healthy cycles of behavior. Literacy is not merely an education; it is a source of liberation.

As a kindergarten teacher, I am often asked how it is possible to teach young children to embrace the transformative power of books to heal. "They can't even read," people often say. (Five-year-olds can, in fact, read, but I'll refer you to the work of early literacy experts such as Matt Glover and Kathy Collins for more on that.) I wonder how it is even possible to teach young children, especially those who experience trauma, to read without such considerations. Of what value is teaching children to isolate the initial and final consonants in words if we do not teach them to find and lose themselves and their worlds—those in which they live and those they imagine—in books?

Moved by the work with young children in Reggio-inspired Opal School in Portland, Oregon, we spend a lot of time "cracking open" words in order to enhance our thoughts in our classroom. After all, Vygotsky wrote, "Language is the tool of thought." Rather than isolating and defining words outright for them and swimming on the surface of those words, I carefully curate collections of texts of various genres that provide children with an invitation to engage deeply in uncovering their themes and exploring words within and related to those rich texts.

We recently read *Those Shoes*, *Knuffle Bunny Free*, *Maddi's Fridge*, and *The Giving Tree* within a week. As I anticipated, these beautiful picture books led us to consider the Golden Rule. Through no fault of their own, many of my students often find themselves amidst conflict and are required to deplete themselves to salvage their relationships with children and adults alike. So I set them up to wonder whether or not the Golden Rule applies to every situation. *Does giving have limits? Are some things too sacred to part with? Is there a difference between giving away something that we have an abundance of or can replace, and something we only have one of or that is irreplaceable? How about giving away something we care deeply about versus something for which we do not have strong feelings? What words do we use to talk about these ideas?* These are the questions we pondered throughout that week.

Though the conversation was lively, deep, and sometimes even heated, the most powerful response to this inquiry took place the following week during a walk around our school's campus. After taking a close look at several branches that had fallen from a large tree and chasing a butterfly, we dared to walk through a somewhat hidden area of our front lawn we had never explored before. As we navigated the tiny space, one child discovered that some flowers had fallen from a bush and picked them up to take back to our classroom. Just as we thought we had experienced enough and turned to walk away, another child uncovered a plaque beneath a tree.

"Ms. J, what does all of this say?" she asked.

The entire class gasped audibly as I read the inscription. The tree behind the plaque had been planted in memory of someone who had passed away.

"Is she under there?" one student asked.

"Is this where she's buried?" asked another.

The children had more questions, I'm afraid, than I did answers. They carried on, pondering death and remembering their loved ones the way kindergarteners are wont to—sans fear.

One student knelt down and used her bare hand to clean off the plaque, insisting that it was a way to honor the dead. "We need to keep this clean for her."

Another student, the one who'd picked up the flowers, bent over and gently placed them on the plaque. "She needs flowers."

This walk was quickly becoming a memorial service without the comforting words.

When we began to walk away, a student tapped me, looked back at the memorial tree and said, "Ms. J, this is a giving tree. It has so much love for that lady like the other tree loved the boy. . ."

As professional educators, we have a lot of power. We can use it to limit children to our narrow paradigms, or we can respect their intellectual capacity and fullness as human beings and invite them to co-create a cultural landscape in our classrooms wherein books are valued as friends.

We can model, even with our youngest readers, through thoughtful read-alouds, how our book friends render feelings of comfort and joy and provide safe spaces within which children and adults alike can find independence, interdependence, and growth. As one of my students said, "Reading is better than food." And that is why its heaviness is so bearable.

# Closing Thoughts

Together, we can make a difference in the lives of children by ensuring that every child has abundant opportunities to connect with books, build empathy, forge relationships with others, and develop the literacy skills they need to reach their full potential. Given time, access, choice, and community, more children will become readers. Thank you for everything you do to support the reading lives of young people in your community.

# References

Adams, M. J. (2006). The promise of automatic speech recognition for fostering literacy growth in children and adults. In M. C. McKenna, L. D. Labbo, R. D. Kieffer, & D. Reinking (Eds.), *International Handbook of Literacy and Technology, Volume 2*. Mahwah, NJ: Lawrence Erlbaum Associates.

Alexander, K. L., Entwisle, D. R., & Olson, L. S. (2007). Summer learning and its implications: Insights from the Beginning School Study. In R. Fairchild & G. C. Noam (Eds.), *Summertime: Confronting risks, exploring solutions.* (Vol. 114, pp. 11–32). San Francisco: Jossey-Bass.

Allen, J. (2000). *Yellow brick roads: Shared and guided paths to independent reading 4–12.* Portland, ME: Stenhouse.

Allington, R. L. (2014). How reading volume affects both reading fluency and reading achievement. *International Electronic Journal of Elementary Education, 7*(1), 13–26. Retrieved July 2, 2018, from files.eric.ed.gov/fulltext/EJ1053794.pdf

Allington, R. L., & Gabriel, R. E. (2012). Every child, every day. *Educational Leadership, 69*(6), 10–15. Retrieved July 1, 2018, from www.ascd.org/publications/educational-leadership/mar12/vol69/num06/every-child,-every-day.aspx

Allington, R., Guice, S., Michaelson, N., Baker, K., & Li, S. (1996). "Literature-based curricula in high-poverty schools." In M. F. Graves, P. van den Broek, & B. Taylor (Eds.), *The first R: Every child's right to read.* New York: Teachers College Press: 73–96

Allington, R. L., & McGill-Franzen, A. (2013). *Summer reading: Closing the rich/poor reading achievement gap.* New York: Teachers College Press.

American Library Association. (2011, July 18). Position statement on labeling books with reading levels. Retrieved June 30, 2018, from www.ala.org/aasl/advocacy/resources/statements/labeling

Bishop, R. S. (1990). Mirrors, windows, and sliding glass doors. *Perspectives, 1*(3), ix–xi.

Carnoy, M., & Rothstein, R. (2013, January 28). What do international tests really show about U.S. student performance? Retrieved June 30, 2018, from www.epi.org/publication/us-student-performance-testing/

Children's Defense Fund. Ending child poverty now. (2015, January 28). Retrieved June 30, 2018, from www.childrensdefense.org/policy/endingchildpoverty/

Clark, C., & Poulton, L. (2011, May 11). Book ownership and its relation to reading enjoyment, attitudes, behaviour and attainment. Retrieved July 1, 2018, from literacytrust.org.uk/research-services/research-reports/book-ownership-and-its-relation-reading-enjoyment-attitudes-behaviour-and-attainment/

Clark, C., & Teravainen, A. (2015). Teachers and literacy: Their perceptions, understanding, confidence and awareness. *National Literacy Trust*. Retrieved July 1, 2018, https://literacytrust.org.uk/research-services/research-reports/teachers-and-literacy-2015-their-perceptions-understanding-confidence-and-awareness

Cooperative Children's Book Center School of Education, University of Wisconsin-Madison. (2018, February 22). Publishing statistics on children's books about people of color and First/Native Nations and by people of color and First/Native Nations authors and illustrators. Retrieved July 1, 2018, from ccbc.education.wisc.edu/books/pcstats.asp

Council of Early Childhood Pediatrics. (2014). Literacy promotion: An essential component of primary care pediatric practice. *Pediatrics, 134*(2), 404–409. doi:10.1542/peds.2014-1384

Crowder, T. (2017, February 23). We are responsible for all readers. Retrieved June 30, 2018, from www.scholastic.com/bookfairs/readerleader/weareallresponsible-022317

Cunningham, A. E., & Stanovich, K. E. (2003). Reading matters: How reading engagement influences cognition. In J. Flood, D. Lapp, J. Squire, & J. Jensen (Eds.), *Handbook of research on teaching the English language arts* (Second Ed.) (pp. 666–675). Mahwah, NJ: Lawrence Erlbaum Associates.

Daniels, H., & Ahmed, S. K. (2015). *Upstanders: How to engage middle school hearts and minds with inquiry.* Portsmouth, NH: Heinemann.

Deci, E. L., Koestner, R., & Ryan, R. M. (2001). Extrinsic rewards and intrinsic motivation in education: Reconsidered once again. *Review of Educational Research, 71*(1), 1–27. doi:10.3102/00346543071001001

Delpit, L. D. (2006). Other people's children: Cultural conflict in the classroom. New York: The New Press.

Delpit, L., & Dowdy, J. K. (2008). *The skin that we speak: Thoughts on language and culture in the classroom.* New York: The New Press.

Dwyer, J. (2017, May 05). Libraries are fining children who can't afford to be without books. Retrieved June 30, 2018, from www.nytimes.com/2017/05/04/nyregion/library-fines-children-books.html

Emdin, C. (2017). *For white folks who teach in the hood… and the rest of y'all too: Reality pedagogy and urban education.* Boston, MA: Beacon Press.

Evans, M., Kelley, J., Sikora, J., & Treiman, D. J. (2010). Family scholarly culture and educational success: Books and schooling in 27 nations. *Research in Social Stratification and Mobility, 28*(2), 171–197.

Fleming, J., Catapano, S., Thompson, C. M., & Carrillo, S. R. (2016). *More mirrors in the classroom: Using urban children's literature to increase literacy.* Lanham, MD: Rowman & Littlefield.

Fountas, I., & Pinnell, G. S. (1996). *Guided reading.* Portsmouth, NH: Heinemann.

Gambrell, L. B., Palmer, B. M., Codling, R. M., & Mazzoni, S. A. (1996). Assessing motivation to read. *The Reading Teacher, 49,* 518–533.

Garcia, A., & O'Donnell-Allen, C. (2015). *Pose, wobble, flow: A culturally proactive approach to literacy instruction.* New York, NY: Teachers College Press.

Gee, J. P. (2000). Identity as an analytic lens for research in education. *Review of Research in Education, 25,* 99–125.

Gilmore, N. (2015, September 17). Nielsen summit shows the data behind the children's book boom. Retrieved July 1, 2018, from www.publishersweekly.com/pw/by-topic/childrens/childrens-industry-news/article/68083-nielsen-summit-shows-the-data-behind-the-childrens-book-boom.html

Guthrie, J. T. (2008). *Engaging adolescents in reading.* Thousand Oaks, CA: Corwin.

Guthrie, J. T., Hoa, A. L., Wigfield, A., Tonks, S. M., Humenick, N. M., & Littles, E. (2007). Reading motivation and reading comprehension growth in the later elementary years. *Contemporary Educational Psychology, 32*(3), 282–313. doi:10.1016/j.cedpsych.2006.05.004

Hack, C., Hepler, S., & Hickman, J. (1993). *Children's literature in the elementary school,* (5th edition). New York: Holt, Rinehart & Winston.

Hammond, Z., & Jackson, Y. (2015). *Culturally responsive teaching and the brain: Promoting authentic engagement and rigor among culturally and linguistically diverse students.* Thousand Oaks, CA: Corwin, a SAGE Company.

Harvey, S., & Ward, A. (2017). *From striving to thriving: How to grow confident, capable readers.* New York: Scholastic Teaching Resources.

Heath, C., & Heath, D. (2017). *The power of moments: Why certain moments have extraordinary impact.* New York: Simon & Schuster.

Hiebert, E., & Reutzel, R. (2010). Revisiting silent reading in 2020 and beyond. *Revisiting Silent Reading: New Directions for Teachers and Researchers,* 290–299. doi:10.1598/0833.17

Holland, D., Lachicotte, W., Skinner, D., & Cain, C. (2003). *Identity and agency in cultural worlds.* Cambridge, MA: Harvard University.

IRA. (2000). Providing books and other print materials for classroom and school libraries: A position statement of the International Reading Association. Retrieved July 1, 2018, from www.literacyworldwide.org/docs/default-source/where-we-stand/providing-books-position-statement.pdf?sfvrsn=e44ea18e_6

Johnson, D., & Blair, A. (2003). The importance and use of student self-selected literature to reading engagement in an elementary reading curriculum. *Reading Horizons, 43*(3). Retrieved July 2, 2018, from scholarworks.wmich.edu/cgi/viewcontent.cgi?article=1155&context=reading_horizons

Kachel, D. E., & Lance, K. C. (2013, March 7). Latest study: A full-time school librarian makes a critical difference in boosting student achievement. Retrieved June 30, 2018, from www.slj.com/2013/03/research/librarian-required-a-new-study-shows-that-a-full-time-school-librarian-makes-a-critical-difference-in-boosting-student-achievement/

Kelley, M. J., & Clausen-Grace, N. (2009). Facilitating engagement by differentiating independent reading. *The Reading Teacher, 63*(4), 313–318. doi:10.1598/rt.63.4.6

Kim, J. (2004). Summer reading and the ethnic achievement gap. *Journal of Education for Students Placed at Risk (JESPAR), 9*(2), 169–188. doi:10.1207/s15327671espr0902_5

Kim, J. S., & Quinn, D. M. (2013). The effects of summer reading on low-income children's literacy achievement from kindergarten to grade 8: A meta-analysis of classroom and home interventions. *Review of Educational Research, 83*(3), 386–431.

Kohn, A. (2010). *Punished by rewards: The trouble with gold stars, incentive plans, As, praise, and other bribes.* Boston, MA: Houghton Mifflin.

Krashen, S. D. (2004). *The power of reading: Insights from the research.* Englewood, CO: Libraries Unlimited.

Krashen, S., Lee, S., & McQuillan, J. (2012). Is the library important? Multivariate studies at the national and international level. *Journal of Language and Literacy Education* [Online], *8*(1), 26–38. Retrieved June 30, 2018 from jolle.coe.uga.edu/wp-content/uploads/2012/06/Is-the-Library-Important.pdf

Lance, K. C., & Kachel, D. E. (2018, June 24). Why school librarians matter: What years of research tell us. Retrieved June 30, 2018, from www.kappanonline.org/lance-kachel-school-librarians-matter-years-research/

Larrick, N. (1965). The all-white world of children's books. *The Saturday Review,* 63–65. Retrieved July 1, 2018, from www.unz.com/print/SaturdayRev-1965sep11-00063

Lifshitz, J. (2018, July 21). On compliance: Shifting the narrative from day 1. Retrieved July 22, 2018, from https://crawlingoutoftheclassroom.wordpress.com/2018/07/21/on-compliance-shifting-the-narrative-from-day-1/

Marinak, B. A., & Gambrell, L. B. (2008). Intrinsic motivation and rewards: What sustains young children's engagement with text? *Literacy Research and Instruction, 47*(1), 9–26. doi:10.1080/19388070701749546

McCarthey, S. J., & Moje, E. B. (2002). Identity matters. *Reading Research Quarterly, 37*(2), 228–238. doi:10.1598/rrq.37.2.6

Messner, K. (2016, September 8). The power of sharing stories in stacks. Retrieved from www.scholastic.com/bookfairs/readerleader/sharingstories-090816

Moje, E. B., Luke, A., Davies, B., & Street, B. (2009). Literacy and identity: Examining the metaphors in history and contemporary research. *Reading Research Quarterly, 44*(4), 415–437. doi:10.1598/rrq.44.4.7

Morrow, L. M., Reutzel, D. R., & Casey, H. (2006). Organization and management of language arts teaching: Classroom environments, grouping practices, and exemplary instruction. In C. Evertson (Ed.), *Handbook of classroom management* (pp. 559–582). Mahwah, NJ: Erlbaum.

Miller, D. (2009). *The book whisperer: Awakening the inner reader in every child*. San Francisco, CA: Jossey-Bass.

Miller, D., & Kelley, S. (2014). *Reading in the wild: The book whisperer's keys to cultivating lifelong reading habits*. San Francisco, CA: Jossey-Bass.

Morrell, E. (2017, June 21). Independent reading: Where we've been, where we're going. Panel presented at Scholastic Reading Summit, Chicago.

Naidoo, J. C., & Dahlen, S. P. (2013). *Diversity in youth literature: Opening doors through reading*. Chicago: American Library Association.

Nagy, W., & Herman, P. (1987). Breadth and depth of vocabulary knowledge: Implications for acquisition and instruction. In M. McKeown & M. Curtiss. (Eds.) *The nature of vocabulary acquisition* (pp. 19–35), Hillsdale, NJ: Erbaum.

NCTE. (2017, May 31). Statement on classroom libraries. Retrieved July 1, 2018, from www2.ncte.org/statement/classroom-libraries/

Neuman, S. B. (1999). Books make a difference: A study of access to literacy. *Reading Research Quarterly*.

Neuman, S. B., & Celano, D. (2012). *Giving our children a fighting chance: Poverty, literacy, and the development of information capital*. New York: Teachers College Press.

Neuman, S. B., & Moland, N. (2016). Book deserts: The consequences of income segregation on children's access to print. *Urban Education*. 10.1177/0042085916654525.

Nicolas, S. (2018, April 10). 50 of our favorite library quotes about how awesome libraries are. Retrieved June 30, 2018, from bookriot.com/2018/03/08/library-quotes/

Parrott, K. (2017, October 17). Fountas and Pinnell say librarians should guide readers by interest, not level. Retrieved July 1, 2018, from www.slj.com/2017/10/literacy/fountas-pinnell-say-librarians-guide-readers-interest-not-level

Platt, C. (2017, October 19). NYC libraries announce fine forgiveness for kids and teens. Retrieved June 30, 2018, from www.nypl.org/blog/2017/10/19/fine-forgiveness

Scholastic kids and family reading report. (2016). Retrieved July 1, 2018, from www.scholastic.com/readingreport/index.htm

Schwanenflugel, P. J., & Knapp, N. F. (2017, February 28). Three myths about "reading levels". Retrieved July 1, 2018, from www.psychologytoday.com/us/blog/reading-minds/201702/three-myths-about-reading-levels

Short, K.G., & Fox, D.L. (2004). The complexity of cultural authenticity in children's literature: A critical review in 53rd Yearbook of the National Reading Conference. Oak Creek, WI: National Reading Conference, Inc.

Souto-Manning, M., Llerena, C. L., Martell, J., Maguire, A. S., & Arce-Boardman, A. (2018). *No more culturally irrelevant teaching*. Portsmouth, NH: Heinemann.

Swan, E., Coddington, C., & Guthrie, J. (2010). Engaged silent reading. In E. Hiebert & R. Reutzel (Eds.), *Revisiting silent reading: New directions for teachers and researchers*. Newark, DE: International Reading Association, 101.

Tatum, A. W. (2009). *Reading for their life: (re)building the textual lineages of African American adolescent males*. Portsmouth, NH: Heinemann.

Tatum, B. D. (2017). *"Why are all the black kids sitting together in the cafeteria?": And other conversations about race*. New York: Basic Books.

Taylor, J. (2009, October 19). Parenting: Decision making. Retrieved July 2, 2018, from www.psychologytoday.com/us/blog/the-power-prime/200910/parenting-decision-making

USDE. (2017). NAEP Mathematics and reading highlights. Retrieved July 1, 2018, from www.nationsreportcard.gov/reading_math_2017_highlights/

Wigfield, A., Mason-Singh, A., Ho, A., & Guthrie, J. (2014). Intervening to improve children's reading motivation and comprehension: Concept-oriented reading instruction. *Advances in Motivation and Achievement*. 18. 37–70. 10.1108/S0749-742320140000018001.

Worthy, J., & McKool, S. (1996). Students who say they hate to read: The importance of opportunity, choice, and access. In D. J. Leu, C. K. Kinzer, & K. A. Hinchman (Eds.), *Literacies for the 21st century: Research and practice. 45th yearbook of the National Reading Conference* (pp. 245–256). Chicago: National Reading Conference.

Worthy, J., & Roser, N. (2010). Productive sustained reading in a bilingual class. In E. Hiebert & R. Reutzel (Eds.), *Revisiting silent reading: New directions for teachers and researchers*. Newark, DE: International Reading Association.

# Contributor Bios

**Sara K. Ahmed** is a literacy coach at NIST International School in Bangkok, Thailand. She has taught in urban, suburban, public, independent, and international schools, where her classrooms were designed to help students consider their own identities and see the humanity in others. Sara is the author of *Being the Change: Lessons and Strategies to Teach Social Comprehension* and co-author with Harvey "Smokey" Daniels of *Upstanders: How to Engage Middle School Hearts and Minds with Inquiry*.

**Jarred Amato** is a high school English teacher in Nashville, Tennessee, and the founder of Project LIT Community. He is passionate about improving literacy attitudes and outcomes. Read his blog at jarredamato.wordpress.com.

**Nicole Barnes** is an elementary media teacher in Wayland, Michigan, with 13 years of experience as an elementary teacher working with 2nd to 4th grade students. Niki enjoys reading and spending time with her family in Kalamazoo, Michigan. You can check out her book blog at daydreamreader.com. Visit scholastic.com/GameChangerResources to read more from Niki.

**Bill Bass** is an Innovation Coordinator for Instructional Technology and Library Media in the Parkway School District in St. Louis, Missouri. As a speaker, writer, and professional developer, he focuses on systemic and sustainable integration of technology into classrooms at all grade levels. Bill has authored two books and currently serves as President-Elect for the ISTE Board of Directors. He was also named one of NSBA's 20 to Watch Leaders in EdTech for 2017.

**Lynsey Burkins** has been a passionate educator for over 13 years in Dublin, Ohio. She resides in Westerville, Ohio with her husband and two children. She is a member of NCTE and writes for The Classroom Communities Blog. She lives for the moment a child sees themself in a book and recognizes that their story matters, too.

**Becky Calzada** is the District Library Services Coordinator in Leander ISD, a fast-growth district located northwest of Austin, Texas. She is a co-moderator for #TXLChat, a weekly Twitter chat for Texas Librarians. Becky is the Region 6 Director for the American Association of School Librarians and a member of the TLA Legislative Advocacy Committee.

**Antero Garcia** is an assistant professor in the Graduate School of Education at Stanford University. He studies gaming, literacies, and youth civic identity and co-founded the Critical Design and Gaming School, a public high school in Los Angeles.

**Brad Gustafson's** life is defined by his faith, family, and desire to help kids (and the educators who serve them) succeed. Brad is a best-selling author, Minnesota Principal of the Year, NSBA "20 to Watch," and national advisor with Future Ready Schools. He serves on Scholastic's Principal Advisory Board and co-hosts UnearthED, a popular school leadership podcast. You can connect with Brad on his blog at BradGustafson.com or via his newest book, *Reclaiming Our Calling*.

**Sue Haney** has been an educator for 26 years. She has been the principal at Parma Elementary School in Michigan for the last 13 years. Prior to her position at Parma, she was a teacher, guidance counselor, and curriculum director in another Jackson County District.

**Maggie Hoddinott** has served as Mamaroneck's Literacy Ambassador since 2015. In this role, she works to ensure all students have rich, literate lives by curating classroom libraries, matching readers with books, and fostering community partnerships. Maggie previously served as a classroom teacher, Reading Recovery teacher, and teacher of deaf/hard of hearing students in the Bronx and Tucson.

**Mary Howard** is a National Literacy Consultant based in Tulsa, Oklahoma, and the author of *RTI From All Sides: What Every Teacher Needs to Know* and *Good to Great Teaching: Focusing on the Literacy Work that Matters*. She has been an educator for 46 years and continues to work in schools across the country. She co-moderates #G2Great weekly Twitter chat @DrMary Howard and shares professional reflections on Facebook as Mary C. Howard.

**Brigid Hubberman,** President of Children's Reading Connection, is an internationally acclaimed community-literacy leader who has shared her expertise and passion for ensuring all children have books to own, and creating a culture of literacy, as far away as Cape Town, South Africa.

**Aeriale Johnson** spends her days learning from young children at Washington Elementary School in San Jose, California. She is a Reggio-inspired educator who knows that literacy empowers children to transform their lives. Aeriale is a Heinemann Fellow, teacher-researcher, and social justice advocate.

**Valinda Kimmel** began teaching three decades ago. She most recently worked as a K–6 instructional coach on an elementary campus in Texas and has begun working as an educational consultant collaborating with teachers, coaches and campus administrators. Valinda is obsessed with matching kids to books so that they'll choose a lifetime of reading. You can check out her site, *Collaborate Innovate Create*, at valindakimmel.com.

**Jennifer LaGarde** is a lifelong teacher and learner, with over 20 years in public education. Her educational passions include leveraging technology to help students develop authentic reading lives and meeting the unique needs of students living in poverty. A huge fan of YA literature, Jennifer currently lives, works, reads, and drinks lots of coffee in Olympia, Washington. Follow her adventures at www.librarygirl.net.

**Jessica Lifshitz** teaches literacy at Meadowbrook Elementary School in Northbrook, Illinois. Each year, she has the absolute privilege of teaching two incredible groups of fifth graders to use reading and writing in order to make the world a better place. She writes about the journey that she and her students take together on her blog at crawlingoutoftheclassroom.wordpress.com.

**Anna Osborn** is a reading intervention teacher at Jefferson Middle School in Columbia, Missouri, and is a member of NCTE and ILA. As a member of the second cohort of Heinemann Fellows, she began doing action research on students' perceptions of themselves as stigmatized readers and blogged about her learning on the Heinemann Blog. A National Board Certified Teacher, Anna is currently pursuing a PhD in reading education at the University of Missouri-Columbia and is interested in continuing research into reader identity.

**LaQuita Outlaw** has been an educator for over 15 years and is currently the principal of Bay Shore Middle School located in Suffolk County, New York. Prior to that, Outlaw was an English Language Arts teacher in Bay Shore and for the NYC Department of Education. She is an adjunct professor at St. Joseph's College, working with graduate students on reading, and shares practical ideas on getting administrators involved in promoting literacy at the building level on Scholastic's Idea Share (www.scholastic.com/bookfairs/idea-share/laquita-outlaw).

**Kimberly N. Parker** currently works with preservice teachers as Assistant Director of Teacher Training at the Shady Hill School in Cambridge, Massachusetts. Kim taught English in public schools for 17 years and served on several committees for NCTE. She was a Heinemann Fellow and her ongoing work explores the literacy lives of Black youth.

**Stacey Riedmiller** is a fourth-grade language arts and social studies teacher from Cincinnati, Ohio. Stacey works to help her thinkers realize that their ideas are important now, and not just when they are grown-ups. Kids truly can change the world!

 **Pernille Ripp** helps students discover their superpower as a former fourth- and fifth- but now seventh-grade English teacher in Oregon, Wisconsin. She opens up her educational practices on her blog www.pernillesripp.com and is also the creator of the Global Read Aloud Project, a global literacy initiative that has connected more than 4,000,000 students. She is an internationally known educational speaker and also the author of several education books. Her latest release is *Passionate Readers: The Art of Reaching and Engaging Every Child*.

 **Kate Roberts** and **Maggie Beattie Roberts** began their teaching careers as middle school teachers in urban centers—Kate in Brooklyn, Maggie in Chicago. After their graduate education at Columbia University's Teachers College, Kate and Maggie became literacy consultants with the Teachers College Reading and Writing Project for a decade. Kate and Maggie now consult, teach, and present nationally in K–12 schools and conferences. Their combined publications include: *Falling in Love with Close Reading* (with Christopher Lehman), *DIY Literacy*, and Kate's most recent publication, *A Novel Approach*, that explores how we can teach whole-class novels while still holding onto student-centered practices.

 **Katherine Sokolowski** has taught for more than 20 years, from kindergarten through seventh grade, and currently teaches seventh grade in Monticello, Illinois. Her thoughts about the power of relationships to engage readers and writers have appeared on NPR, in *Choice Literacy*, and in NCTE's *Voices from the Middle*. Katherine co-facilitates The Nerdy Book Club blog and also writes for the blog Read Write Reflect at readwriteandreflect.blogspot.com.

 **Maria Walther,** who earned a doctorate in elementary education from Northern Illinois University, has taught first grade since 1986. Along with teaching young learners, Maria was honored as Illinois Reading Educator of the Year, and earned the ICARE for Reading Award for fostering the love of reading in children. She has co-authored five professional books and the *Next Step Guided Reading Assessment*. Her latest book is *The Ramped-Up Read Aloud*. Learn more about her books at mariawalther.com. Visit scholastic.com/GameChangerResources to read more from Maria.

 **Annie Ward** has served as the Assistant Superintendent for Curriculum and Instruction for the Mamaroneck Public Schools in Westchester County, New York, since 2004. Prior to that, she was a Local Instructional Superintendent for the New York City Department of Education and the Supervisor of Curriculum and Instruction for the Ridgewood, New Jersey Public Schools. She is the author, with Stephanie Harvey, of *From Striving to Thriving: How to Grow Confident, Capable Readers*.

 **Kristin Ziemke** is an urban school educator and the author of *Amplify: Digital Teaching and Learning in the K-6 Classroom*. Recognized as an international expert in literacy, inquiry, and technology, Kristin works with schools around the world to develop learning experiences that are student-centered, personalized, and authentic. Kristin is an Apple Distinguished Educator, National Board Certified Teacher, and Chicago Council on Global Affairs Emerging Leader.

 **Kyle Zimmer** is president, chief executive, and co-founder of the nonprofit organization First Book, which provides brand new, high quality books for children in need. Kyle's commitment to innovation and collaboration has earned her a reputation as a social sector leader. She serves on the Youth Venture Board of Directors and as a member of the board for James Patterson's ReadKiddoRead, one of the largest get-kids-to-read movements in the country.

# Acknowledgments

It is going to take all of us to equitably increase young people's access to books and support their reading development. Every day, we encounter incredible advocates who are striving to improve the reading lives of children in their schools and communities. We appreciate all of the groups and individuals who have supported this project with their enthusiasm and talents.

Special thanks to our contributors who offered powerful testimonials and suggestions for supporting children and families, providing meaningful book access, and creating thriving reading cultures. Your words show that providing equitable book access and relevant literacy opportunities for all children is attainable, and that each of us plays a role.

Thank you to our Scholastic editorial and design teams—Ray Coutu, Danny Miller, Sarah Longhi, Shelley Griffin, Molly Bradley, Brian LaRossa, and Maria Lilja. Special thanks to our editor, Lois Bridges, for her encouragement and expertise. Lois, we don't know when you sleep! We are grateful to the Scholastic Book Fairs team for their support, especially Robin Hoffman, Anne Wissinger, and John Schumacher.

Special thanks to Marta Perez for the fantastic photo shoot at Parma Elementary and principals Dr. LaQuita Outlaw and Sue Haney for inviting photographers into their schools to share their reading communities.

We are grateful to Kristin McIlhagga, Lynsey Burkins, Jennifer LaGarde, and Valinda Kimmel for reading specific passages or chapters and providing feedback about the text's accuracy and terminology. Any errors or omissions are our responsibility.

Our agent, Molly O'Neill, has been a fantastic sounding board, go-between, and cheerleader for this book. Thank you for the gentle reminders about deadlines and your encouragement to dream big.

We also want to thank Cindy Minnich and Katherine Sokolowski for managing Nerdy Book Club on a daily basis and supporting our other projects online and off. We thank all of the educators and families who read our work, attend our events, and share our ideas. We are honored to be part of a larger community working to engage young people with reading.

We can never adequately thank our spouses, Don and Alaina, and our children for keeping our home lives going while we research and write, and supporting our work— even when it takes us away from home.

Most of all, we would like to thank our students and their families for what you have taught us about children and reading. Thank you for allowing us to share your stories with others. You have taught us more than anyone else.

*Game Changer! Book Access for All Kids*

# Index